קָרוֹב לְכָל קֹרְאָיו

Karov L'chol Korav
For All Who Call:
A Manual for Enhancing the Teaching of Prayer

by Rabbi Jeff Hoffman &
Andrea Cohen-Kiener

Melton Research Center for Jewish Education

Copyright ©2000 by The Melton Research Center
of the Jewish Theological Seminary of America.
All rights reserved. No part of this book may be
reproduced in any manner without the written
permission of The Melton Research Center.

Published by the Melton Research Center
of the Jewish Theological Seminary of America
3080 Broadway, New York, NY 10027

ISBN 1-929419-03-1

MANUFACTURED IN THE UNITED STATES OF AMERICA

Acknowledgements

How shall we thank and acknowledge the people who helped us learn how to pray? In those moments when we experience ourselves in the presence of our Creator, everything we are and all we have ever been is part of that precious Oneness. And for this there are no words. So we begin by offering our thanks to All, to the Holy One of Blessing for sustaining us alive to this moment.

We are students of a long tradition; we have received so much from the living models of our teachers, who have broadened their own relationships with God and shared with us the richness of that journey. We are deeply grateful to these colleagues and teachers, whose spirit and words help inform these pages.

We both wish to thank Heather Feidler, Drew Alexander and Rabbi Eliezer Diamond who reviewed the manuscript at various stages of production. Their insight and comments helped us create a more profound and more useful document.

For our teachers and their students and the students of their students, we ask for peace and lovingkindness, length of days and divine support.

Rabbi Jeff Hoffman:

While I was a rabbinical student at the Jewish Theological Seminary, especially two members of the faculty, Rabbis Neil Gillman and Harlan Weschler, fanned the flame of my spirit. Rabbi Gillman has continued to be a mentor. Also during rabbinical school, I hungrily devoured the writings of Rabbi Abraham Joshua Heschel, who had passed away before I entered the Seminary. His insights and inspiration continue to nurture me. Rabbi Daniel and Hannah Tiferet Siegel opened me to the wisdom found in the movement for Jewish Renewal, and I am thankful to them for that. I am also grateful to Dr. Steve Brown of the Melton Research Center for Jewish Education. I have long viewed his educational commentary on the siddur, *L'eila L'eila: Higher and Higher* as the best introduction available in English to the heart of Jewish prayer. I also want to thank Rabbi Eliezer Havivi from whom I first learned the exercise on Birkat Harotzeh B'teshuvah many years ago at Camp Ramah in the Berkshires.

Finally, I express my thanks and love to my family: my wife Laurie, my children Shaia, Shulie, and Yossi. They have placed a permanent smile on my soul.

Andrea Cohen-Kiener

I am so grateful to the many individuals and institutions that share the task of making the awareness of God a palpable presence in all lives. Their work inspires me, their teachings nurture me, and their companionship sustains me:
Reb Zalman Schachter-Shalomi, shlita
Reb David Wolf-Blank, of blessed memory
Rabbi Shefa Gold, shlita
Rabbi Shlomo Carlebach, of blessed memory
Latifa Kropf, Miriam Minkoff, Hannah Tiferet Seigel, Rabbi David Zaslow, Sara Shendelman, Shlomo Vile, Lev Freidman, Rabbi Ayla Grafstein, Rabbi David Cooper, Rabbi Marcia Prager, David Schneyer, Rabbi Arthur Waskow, Rabbi Jeff Roth, Dr. Ronald C. Kiener, Rabbi Daniel Seigel, and Jessica Weber.

A number of artists inspired or shared specific songs or exercises. We are grateful for their generosity of spirit. Latifa Kropf shared her teachings on sacred dances. We have included her instructions and one very simple dance from her book *Jewish Sacred Dances*. The

Acknowledgements

Tehora He Guided Meditation on Forgiveness was donated by Rabbi David Cooper (*Renewing Your Soul*, pages 38 & 39; HarperSan Fransisco; 1995) The songs: "The Morning Will Unfold for Us," "Baruch She-amar," and "Elohai Neshama" were written by Rabbi Shefa Gold. Hannah Tiferet Seigel wrote the music for "Barechu Dear One" and The "Kedushah Dance". Rabbi David Zaslow created the song "The One." Lev Freidman wrote the music for the Three-Part Shema. David Freidman created the sephirotic diagram "Ten Spheres of Nothingness - Thirty Two Paths of Wisdom". Rabbi Shaya Eisenberg first taught me The Shield Meditation (it's come in handy a number of times!). Anne Brenner submitted her poem Mourning for Peace. Rabbi Jane Kanarek taught us the Amidah writing exercise at Camp Ramah in New England. Shlomo Vile created and shared a number of exercises around his concept of the Jewish Spiritual Tool Box, that is, our prayer accessories: tallit, tefilin and shofar. Rabbi David Wolf-Blank of blessed memory shared with us a number of the graphics and much inspiration.

I wish to thank the staff of the following institutions for allowing me to pilot the materials in this manual with their students: Camp Ramah of New England, Ezra Academy of New Haven, Heritage Academy of Springfield MA, Solomon Schechter of West Hartford, and Temple Beth Shalom of Manchester CT.

I had the distinct pleasure of creating an audiotape to teach some of the songs and chants that are included in this manual. The staff of TapeWorks studio in Hartford Connecticut, Doug Kupper and Bill Ahearn, were tremendously helpful. Our impromptu chorus consisted of Suri Levow-Kreiger, Peninah Adelman, Karin Mondshein, Sara Kiener, Ariana Kiener, Hannah Weitzer, and Lisa Grant.

Dr. Steve Brown, our project director, is a visionary educator. He empowered us, he prodded us and he kept the goal clear for all of us as we developed this truly groundbreaking material. I am grateful for his vision and his courage.

Lisa Grant was the glue for this project. She brought Jeff and me together, she (literally) held my hand through several bouts of writers block and other emotional maladies. She kept the process moving along with grace at every point. Her love for the project, her broad wisdom and her fine hand at editing were indispensible ingredients in the final work.

TABLE OF CONTENTS

Acknowledgements 3

Introductions

The Goals of Jewish Prayer 9
The Mystical Approach in Jewish Prayer 11
A Personal Introduction - ...And You Can, Too 13
Coming Home to Jewish Spiritual Practice 16
Outline by Technique 17

How to use this Manual

Emotional-Conceptual-Spiritual
Stations of the Service 22
Getting Past Self-Consciousness 23
Tips for Teaching Songs and Chants 23
Closing Activities 24
Movement 24
Kavanah 25
Making a Circle
(A group-building lesson plan) 25
Energy Tips 26
A Note on Halacha 26

Guidelines on the Use of Meditations and Visualizations

Tone of Voice 27
Speed of Speech 27
Breath Meditation: Relaxation Breathing Exercise 28
Relaxation Exercise: Repeating a Biblical Phrase 29

Birchot Ha-shachar

Shiviti Breath Meditation 32
Modeh Ani: Bless this Day Guided Meditation 34
Modeh Ani Discussion Guide 36
Tallit as a Robe of Light Guided Meditation 38
Tallit as Blankie 39
The Tallit as Divine Protection
    Discussion Method 40
    Drawing Method 40
Ratzon Meditation 41
Kavanot for Wearing the Tefilin 44
Mah Tovu Section
    Tallit Dance 48
    The Bridge 48
    Gathering Meditation 48

BIRCHOT HA-TORAH TEACHING AND LEARNING EXPERIENCE

TORAH INSIGHTS 50
ELOHAI NESHAMAH - A CHANT 52
THE MORNING WILL UNFOLD FOR US 54
FREE-FORM BIRCHOT HA-SHACHAR (STYLIZED MOVEMENTS) ... 56
    ADULT INTERPRETIVE BIRCHOT HA-SHACHAR 58
    YOUTH VERSION 59

PESUKEI D'ZIMRAH

CACOPHONOUS DAVENNING EXERCISE 60
BARUCH SHE-AMAR CHANT & SING-LANGUAGE 62
ELOHAI SACRED DANCE & CHANT 65
THE ILLUSTRATED ASHREI 66
INTERPRETIVE TRANSLATION OF THE ASHREI 67

SHEMA & HER BLESSINGS

BARCHU, DEAR ONE 68
YOTZER OR: THIS LITTLE LIGHT OF MINE 69
THE KEDUSHAH DANCE 70
AHAVAH RABBAH AND V'AHAVTA: A DRAWING EXERCISE ... 73
KAVANAH BEFORE THE SHEMA 74
GUIDED MEDITATION ON THE 6 CORNERS OF THE SHEMA ... 76
THREE PART SHEMA ROUND & DANCE 78
V'AHAVTA: A SIGN-LANGUAGE EXERCISE 80
SHEMA IN A SUMMER CAMP OR OVERNIGHT SETTING 83
IF SHEMA IS THE ANSWER, WHAT IS THE QUESTION? 84
DERECH EDUT: DRAWING/WRITING EXERCISE 85
THE ONE: A SONG & DANCE 87
TWO ROLE-PLAYING EXERCISES ON THE FIRST LINE OF THE SHEMA
    PLAYING MOSES 88
    TELL YOUR NEIGHBOR 89
THE EXTENDED SHEMA 90
CREATIVE TRANSLATIONS OF THE SHEMA 90
LIVING OUT THE MESSAGE OF THE SHEMA (EMET V'YATZIV)
    DISCUSSION METHOD 92
    DANCE MEDITATION METHOD 93
GA'AL YISRAEL: A DISCUSSION GUIDE 95
PERSONALIZED HASHKIVEYNU BLESSING ACTIVITY 97

THE AMIDAH

AMIDAH CREATIVE WRITING PROJECT 99
AFFIRMATIONS FROM THE AMIDAH (DISCUSSION GUIDE) 100
STEPPING INTO THE PRESENCE OF GOD:
MOVEMENT BEFORE THE AMIDAH 103

Avot and Imahot Visualization	106
Bowing at the Beginning and at the End of the First Bracha: Purposeful Movement	108
Mechalkel Chayim Bechesed	112
The Kedushah I: Word Repetition/Guided Meditation	115
The Kedushah II: Word Repetition/Guided Meditation	119
Birkat Chonen Ha-da'at: Guided Meditation	123
Birkat Ha-rotzeh B'tshuvah: A Writing Exercise in Teshuvah	127
Harotzeh B'tshuvah - Guided Meditation on Forgiveness	129
Birkat Rofeh Cholei Amo Yisrael: A Guided Visualization	131
Healing Meditations - Misheberach L'cholim	133
Korbanot Meditation - For Adults and Teens	135
Purposeful Movement: Modim Anachnu Lach	137
Birkat Kohanim Stylized Movements & Chant	141
Birkat Sim Shalom: A Drawing Exercise On the Letters	143

HALLEL, KRIYAT HA-TORAH & CLOSING PRAYERS

The Dancing Halleluyahs	146
Thematic Aliyot La-torah	147
Aleynu Blessing Circle	149
Shalom Dance & Chant	150
Kavanah before Kaddish Yatom	152
Mourner's Kaddish - Visualization on the Inner Smile	153
Shofarot: Listening with Intention	155

THE SHABBAT TABLE & HOME BLESSINGS

Hadlakat Nerot/Candle Lighting - A Standing Meditation	157
Imahot Meditation/Matriarch's Meditation	158
How to Give a Blessing	159
Kiddush for Shabbat Evening: A Guided Meditation on Releasing	160
Ha-motzi, The Mystery in the Wheat: An "Eating" Exercise	
A Brief Question and Answer Session on the Origin of Our Bread	163
A Spiritually Conscious Eating of Bread	165
Short Kavanah Before Birkat Ha-mazon	166
La'asok B'divrei Torah/To Soak Up the Words of Torah - A Kavanah	168
New Blessings	170
The Sheild: Kavanah for the "The Helping Professional"	172

Stories
The Earth Is Alive: A Camp Fire Story 173
The Mountain 174
The Bartender and the Rebbe 175
The Hopi and the Hasid 177

Lesson Plans
The Four Worlds A Lesson Plan 179
Notnim Reshut Discussion; Group Dynamics in Prayer 183
God, The Writing Project 185
The Names of God 186
God: The Lesson Plan 188
Mitzvah: The Lesson Plan 193

Integrating the Exercises into Your Synagogue
A Sample Service 194
Transitions: Some Secrets of the Trade 197
The Exercises in an Instructional Setting 199

Gems from the Tradition
Moses Maimonides, The Guide of the Perplexed, III:51 202
Abraham Abulafia, The Book of Eternal Life, MS
Oxford 1582, fols. 51b-53a 203
Reb Kalanymous Kalman Shapira,
Bnai Machshavah Tovah 205
Abraham Joshua Heschel, from God in Search of Man 208

Tefilah Resources
Posters 210
Helpful Books 210
Tapes & Music 211
Healing & Hospice 212
Human Resources 212

About the Authors 213

Introductions

The Goals of Jewish Prayer

*I*n a world which increasingly seduces us with multimedia, high tech, quadraphonic, digitally enhanced surround sound experiences, the parsimonious practice of using the written or uttered word to transport us into another realm of feeling and relationship becomes increasingly difficult for many students and teachers. Judaism's adoption of the scholastic model of interaction between worshiper and received text as the core medium of relating to God is, paradoxically, more available to Jews then ever, and at the same time less compelling than many other modes of self expression and emotional stimuli. This manual is a joyful attempt to help Jewish teachers and students of all ages and settings reclaim our legacy of multidimensional spirituality recognizing the need to involve all the senses and multiple intelligences in the study and personal meaning making needed to fully embrace Jewish prayer and liturgy.

As Rabbi Burt Jacobson wrote in his pioneering work *Teaching the Traditional Liturgy* published by the Melton Research Center in 1971, "No matter how important skills, knowledge, and analytical ability are for this Jewish spiritual life, attitudes are the most important...the development of a child's inner life can and does begin much earlier than is usually suspected, and that a child whose emotions and imagination are left exclusively in the hands of secular education and especially the popular media, will not gain personally from the deep spiritual sensitivities of the Jewish heritage."

This book is an attempt to provide for teachers and students a variety of tools and experiences which build on the central core of our liturgical heritage enabling learners to increase their repertoire of strategies to get closer to God. We have been blessed to join in chorus two extraordinary voices, that of Rabbi Jeff Hoffman and Andrea Cohen-Kiener. Rabbi Hoffman, ordained at JTS and author of an important doctoral dissertation entitled "The Bible in the Prayerbook: A Study in Intertextuality" brings a strong and joyful commitment to Jewish law and traditional practice, guided by centuries of mystical and spiritual practices which have enhanced the Halakhic matbeah shel t'fillah. Andrea Cohen-Kiener brings her own commitment to traditional Jewish practice and worship informed by the experiences and innovations of the Jewish Renewal movement which seeks to help Jews find personal meaning in the glories of our tradition. Together, these two talented educators and poetic souls have created an extensive array of meditations, kavanot, breathing exercises, sacred dance and movement practices, guided fantasies, and lesson plans to help Jews of all ages and religious persuasions get closer to the Source of all Being. They have defined spirituality as the alignment of heart, mind and body, and have included practices very evocative of the multiple intelligences reflected in our variegated learners and teachers. With the traditional liturgy as their starting point they have designed activities reflective of the musical, kinesthetic, inter and intrapersonal, naturalistic, verbal, visual and analytical intelligences enabling all learners to access powerful strategies for making personal meaning from the liturgical legacy of our people. It is our hope that teachers and students will acquire new ways of building personal relationships with God that enhance the printed words of the prayer book.

This manual should be viewed as a supplement to existing curricula and materials for teaching prayer. It comes to enhance, not replace. We publish this first edition as an experimental volume since we will value the feedback from the field in shaping a final edition. The wide variety of exercises and experiences provided should find target

INTRODUCTIONS

audiences in every type of Jewish setting- both educational and spiritual. Where exercises done during the prayer service itself might violate Halakhic strictures on hefsek, (places where the service may not be interrupted) we have so signaled to the reader so that you may decide how to proceed. Sometimes the practice can be taught in the classroom and left to the individual to employ during actual prayer times, other practices are best done as preparation for or enhancement of actual prayer services. Since we hope this material will be helpful to the widest range of North American Jewry, we took the approach of pointing out Halakhic difficulties, while leaving it to the end user to make educational and ideational decisions.

As Director of the Melton Research Center, this book is the fulfilment of a personal dream to broaden and enhance the tools and practices available to Jewish educators who have the sacred duty of inducting Jews into the community of Jewish worshipers. I am deeply grateful for our authors, for the superb educational and editorial skills of Ms. Lisa Grant, the patient and professional design skills of Nina Woldin, and the administrative support of my assistant Lisa Silverstein-Weber. May this volume help young and old, teacher and student, all who call, come closer to the ineffable holiness that is God.

Steven M. Brown
Director, Melton Research Center
for Jewish Education
Summer 1999 / 5759

THE MYSTICAL APPROACH IN JEWISH PRAYER

This manual presents a series of exercises and lessons designed to explore the experiential nature of prayer. Some may suspect that the deeply mystical, meditative and intense nature of prayer reflected in these pages comes from some new perspective, outside of authentic Jewish tradition. Far from being alien to Jewish tradition, mysticism has long been a significant and authentic stream in Jewish life and worship.

In too many places, the sense of the transcendent, the presence of God, is not felt. In too many places, Jewish prayer is taught as if it were merely a libretto of songs whose melodies are to be learned, and whose words are sources for vocabulary lists, and whose passages make up nothing more than texts to be "discussed." But prayer is not merely song. Prayer is not "explained" through understanding the meaning of the Hebrew words and through discussion of concepts. Prayer is, in its essence, experienced. Prayer is an attempt to encounter the presence of God that is always with us.

People across the religious spectrum are becoming increasingly aware of the spiritual dimension in worship. Over the last decade, spirituality has "come out of the closet." It is no longer embarrassing to talk about a true heartfelt longing for God in the context of worship. Concentrating on the experience of God through worship is what mystics do. Mysticism is always involved in an intense way with experiencing God's presence.

Under the influence of rationalism and the scientific revolution, Jewish scholars in the first centuries of modernity tended to downplay the role of mysticism in Jewish history; a classic example is the brilliant Jewish historian Heinrich Graetz.[1] That prejudice came to be addressed by the middle of the twentieth century. Professor Gershom Scholem[2] of the Hebrew University, and his students have shown that mysticism has played a central role in Jewish tradition from the earliest time of the Talmud through the dawn of modernity. They did this in two ways. One was to meticulously trace the study and production of mystical texts that have been a part of tradition in every generation. Secondly, they helped to show that the symbolism and psychology behind the difficult texts of Jewish mysticism were highly developed, imaginative and comprehensible. This was in stark contrast to the prevailing wisdom, which viewed this literature as nonsensical, impenetrable utterings.

The prayer known as the Kedushah can serve as a good example of the way mysticism, especially in Jewish prayer, has been viewed by scholars. The various forms of this prayer all consist of poetic verse surrounding two prophetic texts that describe actual visions of God in God's own abode. This is an intensely mystical Jewish prayer!

Both prophetic texts include heavenly scenes of angels surrounding the throne of God. While previous generations of Jewish scholars could not deny the mystical, experiential nature of this prayer, they did deny its antiquity. They attempted to place it relatively late in Jewish tradition, dating it to the middle ages.

This approach is included in the original 1913 edition of

---

[1] See his 14 volume masterpiece, <u>History of the Jews</u>, which first appeared in German in 1875. The first English edition, which was abridged to a mere 7 volumes, appeared in 1891.

[2] Scholem has published many studies. His most influential is <u>Major Trends in Jewish Mysticism</u>, (New York: Schocken Books, 1941) and reprinted several times since.

the classic history of Jewish liturgy by Ismar Elbogen. In subsequent editions, editors added significant caveats to Elbogen's dating of the Kedushah[3], admitting that while a precise chronology is still not clear, there is no doubt that the Kedushah derives from the early Talmudic period, maybe a thousand years earlier than Elbogen had assigned.

More recent scholarship (the work of Meir Bar-Ilan[4], for example) has shown that the range of mystical worship and practice not only arrived from an earlier age, but also consisted of a more extensive and diverse textual and experiential nature than previously thought. The number of texts of the Kedushah itself is quite impressive. And their function as texts designed to induce a meditative state and, ultimately, visions is unmistakable.

The perspective of this manual is that prayer, in general, is a mystical experience. It is "mystical" because it is designed to have us focus on the presence of God. It is an experience, because it always has been more than the sum of the words of a prayer and its melody. All prayer is meant to help us concentrate on the presence of God. This is a function of prayer that was natural to our ancient ancestors, but that evaded many of us moderns. More and more these days, people have become open to the experiential essence of prayer. The purpose of this manual is to provide guidance in teaching traditional prayer, using this approach. It is our hope that this manual will make a modest contribution towards returning some of the ancient spirit of prayer to modern Jews' worship.

---

[3]See the latest edition, and the first to appear in English: Ismar Elbogen, Jewish Liturgy: A Comprehensive History, trans. by Raymond P. Scheindlein (New York: The Jewish Theological Seminary and The Jewish Publication Society, 1993). The original edition was published in German in 1913 under the title Der judische Gottesdienst in seiner geschichtlischen Entwicklung. The first edition to contain the revisions mentioned is the Hebrew edition published in 1972 under under the title HaTefillah BeYisra'el BeHathutah HaHistorit.

[4]Meir Bar Ilan, The Mysteries of Jewish Prayer and Hekhalot (Hebrew), (Ramat Aviv: Bar Ilan University Press, 1987).

How I Came to Be Comfortable Leading Meditations, Visualizations, and Other Spiritual Exercises in Jewish Prayer, and Maybe You Can Too

By Rabbi Jeff Hoffman

As I write these words, I am sitting at my computer, listening to a CD of a Grateful Dead concert. The music recalls for me many transcendent experiences listening to the music of this quintessential psychedelic rock band (I have always found their music transcendent without the use of additional "aids" of any sort). Some of those experiences were at concerts and some were elsewhere as I listened to tapes on my Walkman, at the banks of the Hudson River, not far from my house.

I am wearing a tie and dress shirt and pants. I am preparing to go to a meeting with another person who is also dressed as a professional. He also, by chance, happens to appreciate the music of the Grateful Dead. This shared interest will help us to discuss what we had agreed to talk about, Jewish mysticism. We have a common experience of being moved beyond words. This kind of feeling is akin to a spiritual experience. This sort of encounter is not confined to a concert hall, or to a house of a worship. The buildings that house the art galleries in my town could work just as well as a potent example. The perches atop nearby bluffs facing the Hudson would do too. To perceive these sorts of things, one doesn't have to be a "holy man" dressed in robes. One can be dressed as a businessman or woman, or in jeans or shorts.

When I say "spiritual experiences," I mean to signify feelings that defy definitive description. They are events that take us out of our physical environment. They activate those parts of our consciousness that work just as well with our eyes closed. They encompass the arenas of art, music, poetry, esthetics in general, and religion. And they point to an existence beyond what we can see with our eyes open. They hint at the presence of God.

My own coming of age as a young adult twenty-five years ago or so initiated a deep interest in both music and Jewish tradition. I know that there are many people who do not associate spirituality with Jewish tradition. Some come from a more Orthodox approach, and complain that they did not discover a spiritual side to religion until it was introduced from an experience with a different religion or from a non-Orthodox, perhaps New Age style of Judaism. Others were brought up with a Reform or non-affiliated experience with Judaism in which a sense of the spiritual might have been present at times in their lives, but it was rarely felt through traditional forms of prayer or other rituals. I was lucky enough to find both tradition and meaning within the Camp Ramah approach to Judaism. During my college years, I was active on campus in what might be called a Ramah-type Jewish experience. I spent a year of college study in Israel and was exposed to Orthodoxy -- both in synagogue, and in my part-time participation at a yeshiva.

I always was attracted to the spiritual side of Judaism, even if it wasn't so close to the surface. Many Jews, both active and disaffected, do not easily link spirituality and Judaism. I always have. I looked for and found the path of spirituality in the tradition of my ancestors. My interest in tradition eventually brought me to the rabbinical school of the Conservative Movement, the Jewish

Theological Seminary. And some fifteen or so years following my ordination from the Seminary, my continuing curiosity in prayer led me to complete a doctorate in Jewish liturgy at the Seminary.

Having said all this, I hasten to add that while I always connected to the spiritual side to whatever Jewish learning or teaching or rituals I have done, most of my participation has been in very conventional, rather than overtly mystical ways. A good part of it has been intellectual. That is certainly true of my doctoral studies. While the content of my doctorate was very spiritual -- Jewish prayer, the form of my study was decidedly dry and academic. While my camp and college davening encounters may have included chanting of niggunim (Chassidic style tunes without words) and very spirited communal singing, they did not include mystical meditations and visualizations. And while my inclusion in Orthodox circles in Israel introduced me to what I consider one form of authentic Jewish dancing -- circling over and over to one or two lines of shouted song repeated hundreds of times, I never heard anyone comment on the mysticism of that moment or attempt to instruct the participants in altering their consciousness through movement.

I did have some contact with New Age or Renewal Judaism while in my first pulpit. My family became close with a couple who has since become well-known as major figures in Jewish Renewal. The husband of this couple and I together studied an early work of Chassidic mysticism as well as the Zohar, the main text of Kabbalah, or Jewish Mysticism. He introduced me to the work of the Zayde of Jewish Renewal, Reb Zalman Schachter-Shalomi. I loved the study, but again, the mode of contact was mostly academic and philosophical, not experiential.

There was one time when the wife of the couple invited me to a Shabbat morning service she was leading in her home. It started late enough for me to join the last section of her worship after the services in my own synagogue had concluded. I remember little of the service itself, but I can't forget one very small aspect of my participation, which nevertheless, I recall with some embarrassment. When I arrived, I noticed that the hallway was littered with pairs of shoes, which the participants had apparently all shed. At that moment, I remembered an Orthodox rabbi once telling me that when I daven I should always have my shoes on. As I entered the small living room where the prayers were being conducted, I remember that she invited me to get comfortable and take off my shoes. I replied somewhat defiantly that no, I'd prefer to keep them on. It was an uncomfortable moment emotionally: Such an insignificant invitation -- "get comfortable, take off your shoes"-- seemed too direct an invitation to join, to be part of the group, right off the bat. It also proved to be an uncomfortable experience physically: Sitting on the floor wearing the stiff, fancy black shoes I had on was ridiculous. But I kept them on.

This is all to say it took some doing on my part to overcome the embarrassment and self-consciousness I felt when I began experimenting with teaching Jewish meditation, visualization, and other Jewish spiritual exercises. I had, on occasion, written my own meditations, especially for terribly stressful times when I found that I just could not daven using the traditional Hebrew liturgy. These were times when I needed to get right to the point, and express my needs to God and to reassure myself of God's closeness in my own words. And I recall my trepidation at sharing those modest paragraphs with friends, and my amazement at the positive response.

I felt similarly possessed with self-doubt before I tested the exercises in this manual with different age groups. The barrier I felt was that I was asking people to do things they were not usually used to doing. It can be hard enough to merely converse about God and spirituality, but to go beyond talking, and to ask people to actually involve themselves in spiritual exercises like meditation and guided movement that they might more readily associate with eastern shamans, or some charlatan spiritual healer than with a Jewish teacher, is a natural obstacle in the path.

How I Came to be Comfortable . . .

From my studies, I know that Jews had not only talked about and studied mysticism for centuries, but had actually practiced mystical exercises for all of our history. I also knew that scholars use the term "Meditative Kabbalah" to refer to the study of Jewish mystical works, and "Ecstatic Kabbalah" to define those personalities and movements which actually engaged in mystical practices such as repeating verses over and over or contemplating the written out name of God after careful preparation, which might include days of fasting.

I knew all these things, but it wasn't until I saw the openness of groups old and young to spiritual exercises I brought them, that I was able to calm my doubts. I have been consistently overwhelmed at the willingness of fifth, sixth, and seventh graders in Hebrew School to participate in guided meditations, at the profundity of the responses of first graders in a Solomon Schechter Day School to their participation in these spiritual exercises, and at the thirst of the teachers whom I've directed in Jewish visualizations at several conferences.

There have been challenges. I've found that students in the years around bar/bat mitzvah need lots of space between them when doing these exercises. And one serious participant in an Adult Education course I taught on Jewish spiritual practices loudly and boldly declared, "What's Jewish about this?! This just doesn't feel Jewish." Well, yes, it is understandable that it doesn't feel Jewish, I told him. We're not used to it. But our ancestors were, there are Jews around the world today that feel very comfortable with it, and we can as well.

We all come with our own particular Jewish background, and our own personal intellectual/emotional make-up, and all of this will influence our comfort-level with leading what may feel like very different, threatening, teaching exercises. My suggestion is: Try it. Try it to the extent you can on your own first. Get as familiar and comfortable with the exercises you intend to share with others. And then, know that many, many people not only are open to this sort of teaching, but so many of us need to know that Jewish prayer and ritual can bring them so close to God!

Coming Home to Jewish Spiritual Practice

By Andrea Cohen-Kiener

Two strong memories, and the sharp contrast between them, shape my early experience of Jewish liturgical life. As a youngster at Camp Ramah in Wisconsin, Friday was a day apart. The girls huddled in cabins all afternoon, setting hair, tying bows, applying sweet perfumes. We graciously loaned scarves and belts and bows and gently adorned each other. Nods of approval came when each of us looked just right. We walked in a studied nonchalance down to the lakefront where we were greeted by the young men of our camp, who also looked fine and smelled fresh. The innocent love shared by the sister-campers and the sweet flush of attention from our male counterparts were a very fitting emotional underlay for the energy of Kabbalat Shabbat. Beauty, affection and a royal demeanor are among the gifts of Shabbat; these gifts were a subliminal reality for us on Friday nights at camp.

The second memory is not so sweet. It was a confusing experience, an exercise in disorientation. I have memories of high holidays with my extended family. People arguing over seats, trying to "knock each other out" by showing up at Yom Kippur services with a stunning new fur coat. I remember debates about where to go for lunch after Yom Kippur services, which were expected to be deadening and boring and most especially "looooong!"

The above description of the high holidays is not, let's be frank, the *official* approach of the Conservative movement but was *my* official Conservative experience. Naturally, I was a little turned off. I had in - my kishkes - a real taste of a Jewish spiritual potential (from camp) and I had - in my head (from Hebrew school) - the official inspiration and wisdom of the Jewish tradition. But I had in my day to day life a serious disconnection; none of the adults I knew practiced Judaism in a sincere and joyful way.

As a teenager, I labeled the whole Jewish enterprise "hypocritical" and left it for the grown ups to sort out. I had more important things to do, ballet class, high school and so on. But I kept showing up at Hebrew school. I remember sitting in a Pirke Avot class in 10th grade (Thank you Rabbi Ettedgui. I turned out okay after all). My mind was on auto-pilot, ready to be bored but my insides were paying attention. In spite of my outer reserve, some of those lessons were imparted directly to my soul.

I believe that a craving for the spirit is a human hunger as real as the need for food. I was getting a little bit of sustenance at the Jewish table but not nearly a balanced diet. So I kept looking. Psychology interested me, especially the transpersonal psychology of the 60's (Ah, the 60's.) Meditation seemed valuable. I learned to chant a few Hindu phrases and kept a good eye up for signs of elephant gods and other alien practices. None presented themselves so I continued to study yoga and a Hindu sitting practice. Sacred movement was appealing. Several traditions from the east were around in those days that brought together simple or complicated movement patterns with a prayer or meditation practice. I was a dancer; these combinations added to my learning about human consciousness.

I continued to study Judaism, finding there a wise sociology and psychology. I hadn't a clue about the spiritual potential of Judaism. No one I saw or knew practiced it! Enter Reb Zalman. Rabbi Zalman Schachter-Shalomi (Shlita/may his years be many and blessed) was a seminal teacher for hundreds of wandering Jews in the 60's and 70's. He was a Lubavitcher who was, to use his words, "pulled into the future" by the teachings of feminism, ecology, the meditative traditions of the East and the earth-based traditions of indigenous people everywhere. Here was a man whose first spiritual language was Jewish who was now multi-lingual. He repeated in thousands of way "You don't have to leave Judaism to have spiritual depth." My years of bifurcating were over. I could now have tribe and spirit on the same menu. Reb Zalman became a teacher and mentor for me. The community he inspired has grown and nourished many people, reaching well beyond the original adherents of Reb Zalman's syncretistic message.

Reb Zalman showed me the door to the spiritual rooms of the palace of Jewish tradition. Since entering those rooms, I have learned from many generations of Jewish teachers about meditation, community, consciousness and prayer, work on self and love. When I first began to know the deep connection between Jewish spiritual teachings and other world traditions, I would excitedly note "Look! We have that in Judaism too!" Now, when I know my own tradition so much more deeply, I encounter profound lessons that seep across tribal and national boundaries to re-appear, slightly rephrased, in Judaism and in other spiritual traditions. When I notice this symmetry now, my inner response is "That is the nature of spiritual teaching. How could it be otherwise?"

I am grateful for my wandering years now, though they were lonely and painful at the time. They prepared me to recognize the depth of Jewish teaching when I was blessed to encounter living embodiments of it. And my wandering years keep me open so that I can recognize gifts of spirit and personal maturity in persons whose outer practice may be very different from my own. I find that the more deeply I understand my tradition, the more interested I am in interfaith dialogue. This seems to me a logical way to practice the credo "God is one."

My understanding of sacred psychology is this: Nothing exists except God. We are in a game of hide-and-seek with that particular piece of information. We are separated from that knowledge by our illusions, our ego, our forgetfulness. Judaism has teachings for us at all stages of our human development. For those of us who are awake to the spiritual yearnings of our nature, Judaism helps us stay alert to the idea that nothing exists except God, in a real, visceral, moment-to-moment way.

The goal of this book is to share with you the teacher, you the seeker and you the transmitter of sacred teachings, tools from the Jewish tradition. May we merit the support of our ancestors and the help of Ha-kadosh Baruch Hu. May we be guided to learn, to teach, to embody and to honor the reality of God in each life.

Outline by Technique

Introductions:

  The Mystical Approach in Jewish Prayer **11**
  Outline by Technique **18**
  How to use this Manual **22**
  Guidelines on the Use of Meditations and Visualizations **27**
  Relaxation Breathing Exercise **28**
  Repeating a Biblical Phrase **29**
  Integrating the Exercises into your Synagogue **193**
  The exercises in an Instructional Setting **199**

Guided Meditations

  Shiviti (a breath meditation on YHVH) **32**
  Bless This Day Guided Meditation
  (visualizing and blessing the day ahead) **34**
  Ratzon Meditation
  (opening visualization on the place of the tefilin) **41**
  Gathering Meditation (for Mah Tovu or putting on the tallit) **48**
  Kavanah before the Shema **74**
  Meditation on the 6 Corners of the Shema **76**
  Avot and Imahot Visualization
  (guided meditation on the Ancestors) **106**
  Birchat Chonen Ha-daat (guided experience on seeking insight) **123**
  HaRotzeh B'tshuvah (guided meditation on forgiveness) **129**
  Korbanot Meditation
  (guided imagery on offering ourselves as instruments of God) **135**
  Kaddish Yatom (a guided visualization on the Inner Smile) **153**
  Kiddush for Shabbat Evening **157**
  Ha-motzi: An Eating Exercise **163**
  Short Kavanah before the Birkat Ha-mazon **166**
  La-asok B'divrei Torah (a guided meditation before Torah study) **168**

Purposeful Movement Meditations

  Stepping Into the Presence of God (introduction to the Amidah) **103**
  Bowing - Purposeful Motion at the first bracha of the Amidah **108**
  Purposeful movement - Modim Anachnu Lach **137**

Meditations: Personal Kavanot

  Tallit as Robe of Light (brief visualization for donning tallit) **38**
  Kavanot for Wearing the Tefilin **44**
  Affirmations from the Amidah - Personal Meditations **100**
  Shofarot: Listening with Intention **155**
  Hadlakat Nerot/Lighting Candles (a standing meditation) **157**
  The Shield (a kavanah for the helping professional) **172**

Outline by Technique

MEDITATIONS: WORD REPETITIONS

- Repeating a Biblical Phrase 29
- Kedushah I 115
- Kedushah II 119
- Rofeh Cholei Amo Yisrael (a healing meditation) 131

BLESSINGS

- Birkat Kohanim Dance & Chant 141
- Thematic Aliyot La-torah 147
- Aleynu Blessing Circle 149
- How to Give a Blessing 159
- New Blessings 170

SONG/MOVEMENT

- Tallit Dance 48
- The Bridge 48
- Elohai Neshama (chant with instructions) 52
- The Morning Will Unfold for Us (repeat-after-me song and movement) 54
- Free-Form Birchot Ha-shachar (group created movement activity) 56
- Cacophonous Davenning Exercise 60
- Baruch She-amar Chant & Sign Language 62
- Elohai Sacred Dance and Chant 65
- Barchu, Dear One (repeat-after-me song and movement) 68
- Yotzer Or: This Little Light of Mine 69
- The Kedushah Dance (three part song with movement) 70
- Three Part Shema (song with movement) 78
- V'ahavta: A Sign Language Exercise 80
- The One (song and free-form dance) 87
- Living Out the Lessons of the Shema (a dance meditation) 93
- The Dancing Halleluyahs (free-form dance) 146
- Shalom Chant & Stylized Movement 150

RESOURCES

- Gems from the Tradition 202
- Posters 210
- Books 210
- Tapes 211
- Musical Instruments 211

LESSON PLANS

- Creative Translations of the Shema 90

Outline by Technique

    Making a Circle - Lesson on group building **25**
    Modeh Ani - discussion guide **36**
    Shema in an Overnight or Summer Camp Setting **83**
    Gaal Yisrael - discussion guide **95**
    Shofarot - listening with intention **155**
    The Four Worlds - Theoretical framework
    for spiritual education **179**
    Notnim Reshut - Lesson on self-consciousness
    and group dynamics in prayer **183**
    Names of God **186**
    God: The Lesson Plan **188**
    Mitzvah: The Lesson Plan - Why should I do this stuff anyway? **193**

InterActivity
    Tallit as Blankie (a discussion about feeling protected) **39**
    Tallit as Divine Protection (a discussion) **40**
    Birchot Ha-torah - Learning & Teaching Exercise **50**
    Role-Play on the Shema **88**
    Living Out the Message of the Shema - Discussion Method **92**
    Gaal Yisrael (A Discussion Guide) **95**
    Personalized Hashkiveynu Blessing **97**
    Kavanah before Kaddish Yatom **152**

Writing Activities
    If Shema is the Answer, what is the question? **84**
    Derech Edut **85**
    Amidah Creative Writing Project **99**
    Ha-rozteh B'tshuvah (a writing exercise) **127**
    New Blessings **170**
    God: The Writing Project **185**

Drawing & Art
    Tallit as Divine Protection - drawing method **40**
    The Illustrated Ashrei **66**
    Birkat Sim Shalom: A drawing exercise on the letters **143**

Stories
    The Earth Is Alive **173**
    The Mountain **174**
    The Bartender and the Rebbe **175**
    The Hopi and the Hasid **177**

Hand Outs - Camera Ready

Torah Insights	**51**
Birchot Ha-shachar	
Adult Interpretive Version	**58**
Youth Version	**59**
Interpretive Translation of Ashrei	**67**
Creative Translations of the Shema	**90**
Emet V'yetziv: The Sixteen Attributes of God's Teachings	**94**
Hashkiveynu - Lie Us Down in Peace	**98**
Affirmations from the Daily Amidah	**101**
Mechalkel Chayim	**114**
birkat Chonen Ha-da'at	**126**
Names of God	**187**

How to Use this Manual

This manual is for people who lead and teach tefilah. We have designed the exercises, lesson plans and activities for use in a classroom or informal instructional setting. Depending on the custom of your school or community, some of the exercises can be used within a prayer setting.

Our goal is to help you and your students understand prayer with body, heart and mind. Most of the activities are multi-focal, that is, we have combined techniques that ask you to move or draw or act out the prayers. We believe that by engaging the whole person in a prayer or instructional experience, the message of the prayer is felt and remembered more deeply. The Four Worlds Lesson Plan (PAGE) gives the Jewish psychological and spiritual framework for this approach. The Modeh Ani Lesson Plan (PAGE) helps present these ideas to your students. These two are good starter activities for groups.

The manual includes a variety of techniques to help you and your students study and experience the prayers more fully. Not all of these techniques will be suitable for all instructors and all students. We have given some guidance as to the best age group and settings for various activities, but your unique likes and dislikes as a person must be taken into account! If you have a deep love for drama or music or silent prayer or sign language, your enthusiasm and joy will be communicated to the students. If on the other hand, you are uncomfortable with art materials or movements or meditation, this too will be felt by the group. It is wiser to use the techniques that you find useful and enjoyable! We hope our guide will encourage you and enable you to widen the tools and techniques that you are comfortable using, but you need to be your own guide.

Essentially, we present a variety of techniques that in some way expand the experience of the words on the page of the siddur. This manual contains a mix and match of techniques and liturgical ideas. Once you feel comfortable with a certain technique, you can apply it in another part of the service. For example, we provide instructions for "Cacophonous Davening" and demonstrate the technique with a selected prayer. You may want to use that style of chanting for another part of the service. Elsewhere, we suggest sign language and other simple motions to embody and express several prayers. If you like these techniques, you can expand your repetoire of prayers that you sign or dance. Toward this end, we offer a few instructions for using the techniques in general before getting started with the specific activities.

Emotional-Conceptual-Spiritual Stations of the Services

Our creative exercises are designed to help people understand the meaning, the feeling and spiritual depth of that section or prayer. Most prayers have a key idea with many sub-themes. An outline of some of the deeper messages in the morning service, for example, look like this:

V'ahavta L're-echa/Opening to love, forgiveness, self-acceptance
Modeh Ani/Gratefulness
Tallit & tefilin/Personal devotions
Mah Tovu/Entering the Prayer Space
Asher Yatzar/Appreciating the body
Birchot Ha-torah/Consciousness/Receiving Torah
Elohai Neshamah/Appreciating the breath of life
Birchot Hashachar/Divine guidance throughout daily life, Waking Into the Body
Yehi Ratzon/Asking for Divine protection
Akeda & Korbanot/Offering ourselves to God's service
Kaddish D'rabanan/Taking note of the consciousness accumulated to this point/transition
Pisukei D'zimrah/Songs of praise, various themes

How to Use this Manual

Chatzi Kaddish/Taking note of the awareness generated to this point/transition
Barchu/Gathering as a community for Prayer
Yotzer Or/Blessing on Light
Ohev Et Amo/Blessing on Love
Shema/Proclaiming the Oneness, Feeling our connections
Geulah/Feeling the power of salvation/liberation
Hashkiveynu/Asking for God's Protection
Adonai Sefatai Tiftach/Preparation for the Amidah
Amidah/The Credo, various themes
Elohai Netzor/Personal prayers
Tachanun/Recognizing our smallness
Kaddish/Taking note of the awareness gathered to this point
Reading Torah (Mon & Thurs)/Various themes
Aleynu/Messianic Vision
Shir Shel Yom/Tuning in to daily blessing
Kaddish Yatom/Mourner's recitation, Honoring our losses, Comforting each other

This list of themes is far from exhaustive! It really is just a set of suggestions to help you see how we created these exercises. You too, with some experience, can generate activities on your own.

Getting Past Self-Consciousness

Ideally, our goal is to bring people into a "shared private moment." Our connection with the divine is personal but most Jewish prayer is communal! A group can consciously agree to support spiritual work. In such a supportive environment, each individual can *unselfconsciously* experience kavanah/intentionality and the states of mind and awareness that are possible. Self-consciousness is an enormous impediment to freedom of expression of spirit, especially for teens and adults.

Often, it is helpful to address this issue explicitly. Simply state "We need to feel safe and comfortable with one another, in order to do this activity. Prayer is a subtle thing. We each need to feel sure that no one will find us silly if we daven with feeling." The Notnim Reshut /Group Dynamics in Prayer Exercise, page 180, is a lesson plan that helps a group explore the dynamics of self-consciousness.

Humor is another tool. Gently and playfully, touch upon the subject. Tell adults that you want to daven with their inner child. Or say "You can do this. He's doing it too..." You can ameliorate self-consciousness by starting with creative pieces which are less threatening. Adding a welcoming hand motion during the singing of Mah Tovu, for example, is less risky than a sacred dance. A guided meditation, with eyes closed, is less risky than making up body postures to go with the birchot hashachar/morning blessings. You can introduce "riskier" techniques as your group coalesces and your confidence builds.

Tips for Teaching Songs & Chants

Break the song into sections, first going over the words for pronounciation and meaning. Teach each section separately and go over it several times until the group has mastered that section. Put the sections together. Many of the songs we included are rounds, but you may not be able to do a round the first time you teach the song. Don't push it. Let the group build confidence. IT HELPS A GREAT DEAL WHEN DOING ROUNDS IF TWO PEOPLE HAVE MASTERED THE SONG so that someone is leading each part of the round.

After teaching the song and singing it a few times, stop for a moment, correct the tune or relearn any section that the group is not singing confidently. Remind the group of the meaning of the prayer and what energy or kavanah/intention they want to create with their voices and their minds. Then start again. This pausing to retune often has a very nice effect on building confidence and kavanah.

Give very clear instructions to the group when you end the song. Slow down or sing more and more softly to indicate the end of a song.

Chanting is a little different than singing. Both create beauty. Both help build group cohesion because they are both group activities. Because of the simple and repetitive nature of chanting, there are some additional factors. When repeating a chant, the group's breathing becomes synchronized. The simple and repetitive nature of a chant allows the mind to slow and clear. In effect, chanting is a singing meditation. One prolific teacher of Jewish chant, Rabbi Shefa Gold, recommends that silence follow a chant. The message and energy of a chant can be absorbed in the silence that follows.

Closing Activities

As you become more comfortable leading groups into a deep personal and spiritual experience, you will begin to sense that there is quite a difference between those elevated states of consciousness and "normal" consciousness. Our siddur brilliantly helps us make the transition back to normal consciousness by inserting some humbling (Tachanun, Aleynu) and sobering prayers (Kaddish Yatom) at the end of a each service. Eating is also a great way to "come down" which is reflected in most of our holiday rituals and Shabbat services that end with a ceremonial meal!

If you use these exercises in a classroom setting, especially the meditations, you will have to re-orient your students so they can continue on to the next class or go off to recess, whatever the case may be. This can be accomplished by some small physical change and by simply naming the fact that a transition is underway. Here are several examples. Again, mix and match to best meet the needs of your particular setting.

After a guided meditation, say: "In a moment, I am going to turn on the lights. Slowly return your attention to the room you are in, to the sounds around you…"

After an energetic song/dance: Give out a big "Amen"
After a meditative song/dance, say: Let's just be still for a moment. Hold your eyes closed just for a moment. Feel the openness. Enjoy it. Feel the light energy moving from your head to your toes. Wiggle your toes. Take a small step. Good. Let's open our eyes."

After a meditation, a good discussion of the experience can be very useful educationally and also serve as a good transition back to a more mundane level of consciousness.

In truth, we don't want to come ALL the way back to a normal level of consciousness! We want to begin to expand our ability to be more aware of God and our own depth more of the time. A nice closure for a meditation might be: "Hold on to the feeling of love/comfort/presence you have at this moment. Imagine yourself in the days ahead. Imagine that you continue to feel this love/comfort/presence. See yourself in the days ahead enjoying this feeling that you are having now. Ken Yehi Ratzon! So may it be! Amen!"

Movement

We present three types of movement activities in this manual: sign language, stylized movement and sacred dance. Here is a brief description of each:

Sign Language: American Sign Language (ASL) is a formal language. Because of the nature of the deaf community, there are many variations and dialects. When "translating" Hebrew into ASL, there are interpretations and variations, as there are with any translation. A local friend who is fluent in ASL can be invaluable as an aid in teaching prayer. Printed resources for Hebrew and religious signing appear in the Resources section at the back of the book (PAGE?). Just one word of caution: Please identify to your students when you are using standard ASL and when you are using stylized motions that you have created. This is simply a courtesy to the deaf community.

Stylized Motions: Stylized motions are simply movements that people make up to express the words of a prayer. We offer several activities using this technique to loosely "dance" a prayer. Stylized movement is a wonderful technique for learning Hebrew words and phrases. It is also a lovely "full-body" activity, age and stage appropriate for young people and equally engaging for adults. Choosing the stylized motion to express various prayers is also a good activity to get the creative juices flowing and to have some fun in a group.

Sacred Dance: Sacred dance is based on stylized movement, but the group does not generate the dances. The sacred dances presented in this manual are deep group meditations composed of a prayerful songs and simple movements. Sacred dances are powerful group activities; the sense of kavanah/intentionality can be very profound. Detailed instructions for sacred dance precede "Elohai" Sacred Dance & Chant on page 65.

Kavanah

Kavanah is from the Hebrew root for orient or aim. The general use of the word indicates the act of paying attention to a prayer or acting intentionally to fulfill a mitzvah. There are several "kavanot," or reminders that were created by individual sages and became incorporated into the liturgy (the phrase recited before the Amidah and the imagery invoked while wrapped in one's tallit are examples).

Most of our exercises can be used to enhance kavanah or intentionality in prayer. Some of the exercises deepen one's ability to pay attention in general. Others provide a sense of what one might want to hold in mind while reciting a certain prayer.

Except for one section of the service (see the note below on halachah), kavanot, brief invocations or introductions, are a methodology that is very easy to incorporate into a service. A brief kavanah before an emotional prayer (the mourner's Kaddish, for example) can build the emotional impact of a service.

Making a Circle - An Opening Lesson Plan

This lesson plan is good for group building. It makes a good first lesson because it sets the ground rules for listening to each other. You can use it as an introduction to sections of the service that talk about communication and having good intentions.

Leader: *A good bit of our learning will take place in this circle. In our discussions about prayer, we will often be talking about feelings and very personal experiences. It is important for us all to feel safe. We want to feel that our whole self can be present. There are a couple of rules for learning in a circle, so we can all feel present and engaged. Let's go through the rules together to see if we can all agree to them. If there is any controversy, we'll apply Rule #6; we'll discuss as a group why or why not certain rules feel useful or necessary.*

Rule #1 Everyone is "in": unless you have a broken leg, you must, physically, be part of the circle.

Rule #2 You can "pass." If a topic is being discussed that is too hot, too close to home of too far off for you, when it's your turn to speak, simply pass.

Rule #3 We try to observe the Jewish rules of speech. No name-calling, no labeling a person in a way that can be identified. "I knew this guy..." is okay; "I knew this guy whose initials are RK, who is wearing green today..." is out! We want to get at the issues, not the personality.

Rule #4 Respect each other's privacy. You are going to talk about topics that may be emotionally sensitive. The point of this sharing is to help each other with our best insight and compassion. It would be very painful if this information was used in any other way.

Rule #5 Listen & Speak. You will learn in this class, as you probably already know, that each of us is really unique. That means that there is no right or wrong answer to a lot of the ideas we will discuss. Speaking your truth, your point of view is the only way you can enrich the group's understanding.

When you hear others speak, even if their ideas sound strange or unreasonable at first, accept it as their truth. Probe it, question it, but do not dismiss it. Shimon ben Zoma teaches us (Pirke Avot 4:1) that we are wise if we learn from everyone.

Rule #6 "Make your case" is a phrase we will use from time to time. It means that there is more than one opinion on the floor, or that there is more than one way to interpret your comment. "Make your case." means say a little more about your intention.

Ask your group if there are other ground rules that are needed. Summarize and solicit approval for the ground rules.

Energy Tips

> *Ideas for closing, amplifying or using the exercises are given in boxes like this one, after the activities.*

A Note on Halachah

Certain exercises in this manual ask participants to make what is called a Hefsek הֶפְסֵק, an interruption, between the blessings. There are junctures in the service when a hefsek is prohibited (between the Barchu prayer and the end of the Amida, between the moment of reciting a bracha over performance of a mitzvah and performing the act, any time during the Kedushah, as examples). Some authorities make broad openings in this law "L'shem chinuch/For the sake of learning." Those scholars would allow a technical hefsek, since the "interruption" would tend to increase the level of understanding and intent of the worshipper. There are people who will choose not to incorporate exercises into those moments of a service where there would be a halachic question. Consult with your rabbi or cantor for the community custom.

Guidelines on the Use of Meditations and Visualizations

The way we "read" a text in worship is very different from the way we read a text for instruction or for pleasure. It is much closer to the way that we read a poem, for example, than how we read a newspaper or a novel. A passage which is encountered repeatedly, perhaps even several times every day is not read especially for the information in it. It is to be re-inspired. Another dimension, unlike the reading of a poem, is that a goal of chanting a prayer text is to evoke for ourselves again and again the sense of the presence of God. The very opposite of the optimum way to "read" a prayer is speed-reading. It follows, then, that slow, focused reading can be an effective way to approach a passage in worship.

Many of the exercises in this manual, are meant to emphasize and dramatize the special way of "reading" a prayer so that the spiritual dimension can be as palpable as possible. There are two very important guidelines for the successful usage of these meditations and visualizations. The first is the speed of reading them, and the second is the tone of voice. Few of us have much experience in the kind of reading necessary in leading groups in these exercises. However, it is not hard to learn this skill. It involves reading very slowly, and in the calmest, most relaxed tone that we can muster.

Some practice is in order before using these exercises with a group.

Tone of Voice

It is easiest to achieve the proper tone when the leader is in a relaxed state.
Therefore, it is recommended that prior to sharing these exercises, the leader prepare in the following way:

1- Try one of the breath or relaxation exercises suggested in the manual, pages 28 - 33.
2- Select any of the meditation or visualization exercises to use in practice. First, regarding tone: Read a line or two of the exercise aloud and pay attention to how your voice sounds.
3- Try to read the same lines again consciously attempting to use the calmest voice possible.
4- A relaxed voice is typically in a lower register relative to your normal speaking voice.
5- Therefore, as those same lines are read again, check your voice -- is it the lowest tone you can use and still be comfortable?

The Speed of Speech

We want to help achieve a prayerful atmosphere by reading slowly, very slowly. One good way to prepare to effectively lead these exercises is to literally time our reading:

1- Sit with a clock or watch that counts seconds.
2- Then, choose a short passage that you know by heart to use as a practice text. It could be a prayer. Many people know the Shema and V'ahavta by heart, for example (Note that we are practicing the pace of our reading not only for the prayers themselves, but for the instructions as well, which are contained in the exercises), or it could be something in English or a very brief monologue that we make up on the spot such as: "I am now practicing the speed of my speaking. I am trying to see how quickly or slowly I am speaking...." You can read into a tape recorder to check the feel and tone of your voice.
3- Time yourself saying whatever text or improvised monologue you've chosen. Time your speaking for ten seconds. As you speak, count the number of words you are saying on your fingers. The leader of a meditation or visualization exercise should optimally be saying ten to fifteen words per ten seconds. That is typically much slower than we are used to in speaking or reading aloud. It requires practice to slow ourselves down.

Relaxation Breathing Exercise*

For all ages
This guided meditation is included on the accompanying tape.

Stand or sit in a comfortable position.
If the group is standing, ask the participants to allow some space between them.

> **Leader:** *We are going to begin with a short meditation to help us relax and get into the right mood for prayer. This whole exercise will only last a few moments.*

The leader continues by saying the following very slowly and calmly. The voice should go down in pitch and intensity:

> *Let's begin by closing our eyes. Close them lightly and comfortably, not tightly. Now, let us focus on our breathing.*
>
> *Pay attention to how often you take a breath.*

Pause for the duration of several breaths.

> *Pay attention to how deep each breath is.*

Pause for the duration of several breaths again.

> **Leader** continuing to speak very slowly and calmly:
> *Now, we want to slow our breathing down just a little bit. Let's see if we can slow our breathing a little.*

Pause for the duration of several breaths.

> *Good. We'll stay in this relaxed state just for another moment or two before we begin to focus on prayer.*

Relaxation Exercise: Repeating a Biblical Phrase*

For all ages
*This guided meditation is included on the accompanying tape.

This is a warm-up exercise designed to help us relax so that we can be in an open mood for prayer. This exercise itself will only last a very few minutes.

> **Leader:** *We are going to repeat a short phrase from the Tanach, the Bible. It was said by a large group of the People of Israel as they gathered on Mount Carmel at the time of Elijah the prophet (I Kings 18:39). At the end of a daylong struggle between Elijah and the priests of Baal, the people were finally convinced that the God of Israel is truly their God. They rejected the idol Baal. Together, they expressed their deep acceptance of God by saying and repeating, "Adonai Hu Ha-elohim, Adonai Hu Ha-elohim," "Adonai is God, Adonai is God." This group expression of faith in God, repeated seven times, is also part of the climactic end of the prayers for Yom Kippur, our holiest day.*
>
> *Reciting this simple line of accepting God and rejecting idols can be a powerful calming and centering experience. When we use this line as a preface for prayer, we do not need to keep in mind the setting of Mount Carmel, or the priests of Baal, or Elijah. We do not even need to concentrate deeply on the meaning of the words. Rather, we should try to let the quiet strength of the words themselves, of the individual syllables, of the sounds, bring us to a state of calm and peace.*

Relaxation Exercise: Repeating a Biblical Phrase

Stand or sit in a comfortable position.
If the group is standing, ask the participants to allow some space between them.

The leader continues by saying the following very slowly and calmly. The voice should go down in pitch and intensity:

> *We are going to recite the phrase "Adonai Hu Ha-elohim" over and over for two or three minutes. We will want to say it very slowly. We should say it only loud enough for our own ears to hear. We should try to recite it with our eyes closed. After a moment or two, it should feel as if we are breathing the words more than saying them. Our goal is to say these words so delicately and quietly, smoothly, calmly, and naturally.*
>
> *We will say the words in a very slow tempo, like this...*

Leader should demonstrate. To do this, it will be necessary first to pause and take in a deep breath and let it out. Then, the leader should recite "Adonai Hu Ha-elohim" slowly, several times, stretching out the sounds. It may help to practice using a watch or clock that displays the seconds. Each of the three words should take five seconds. If we finish saying any of the words in less than five seconds, that is alright as long we then pause silently before saying the next word until five seconds are complete).

> *Let us begin now:*
> *Adonai Hu Ha-elohim.* יי הוּא הָאֱלֹהִים
> *Adonai Hu Ha-elohim.* יי הוּא הָאֱלֹהִים
> *Adonai Hu Ha-elohim.* יי הוּא הָאֱלֹהִים
> *Adonai Hu Ha-elohim.* יי הוּא הָאֱלֹהִים
> *Adonai Hu Ha-elohim.* יי הוּא הָאֱלֹהִים
> *Adonai Hu Ha-elohim.* יי הוּא הָאֱלֹהִים
> *Adonai Hu Ha-elohim.* יי הוּא הָאֱלֹהִים

Relaxation Exercise: Repeating A Biblical Phrase

At some early point into the exercise, maybe a minute into it, the leader should quietly and slowly address and encourage the group by saying either:

"Let's slow it down a little."

"You are doing great."

"As you get used to it, and when you're comfortable, remember to close your eyes as you continue to recite."

After two or three minutes, the leader should say, "O.K., let's get ready to stop reciting... Let's stop now."

> *ENERGY TIP: If the goal is to use this relaxation technique to introduce one of the prayer exercises, the leader may want to ask the group to continue to keep their eyes closed. If the goal is to go into a prayer service in which using the siddur is necessary, the leader may ask the group to slowly open their eyes.*

Birchot Ha-shachar

Shiviti Breath Meditation
For all ages

Shiviti is the Hebrew word for a visual object of meditation, most often a beautifully illuminated picture of the letters of one of the names of God (commonly, yud, heh vav, heh/ י-ה-ו-ה). The idea for this kind of meditation object comes from the Biblical phrase שִׁוִּיתִי י-ה-ו-ה לְנֶגְדִּי תָמִיד/Shiviti Ha-shem L'negdi Tamid/ I constantly face God (Psalms 16:8). Shiviti means "I have placed before me." The following meditation offers God's name, Yud, Heh, Vav, Heh as a basis for a breath meditation.

This meditation can be used as a quieting technique at many points in a service. This exercise, working thoughtfully with Hebrew letters, is also useful for students who are learning the alef-bet. For this and all meditations, give clear instructions and use a calm tone of voice.

> *Leader: We are going to begin this morning by paying attention to our breath. One of God's names, Yud Heh Vav Heh can be seen as a breath, as God's enlivening presence in our bodies. We are going to meditate on the Holy Name, yud, heh, vav, heh. Sit comfortably, evenly, uncross your legs so your blood can circulate freely.* (Allow a moment for people to readjust) *Good.*
>
> *We are in community today yet each of us is going to have a very private experience. Take a moment now to look around. We want to feel that it is okay for us to have a private moment even though we are in a group. No one is going to laugh at you. We will all be trying to pay attention to our inside ideas, not to each other. Give each other permission to enter this very private experience within the group. Good.*
>
> *Let's close our eyes now. Breathe naturally. Let's follow our own bodily rhythm. Notice the flow of the full breath in and out. If our minds start to wander, we'll simply recall our attention to watching the full breath, in and out.*

As we experience each breath, we are going to visualize the letters of the Holy Name as sections of the breath moving through us. The beginning of each breath is the yud: the moment that the breath begins to enter our nose and head. Let each breath begin as a clearing of the nostrils and head. Visualize the yud filling our nostrils, filling our mind (pause 4-5 breaths*). **Good.***

*This yud moves smoothly to the first heh, as the breath moves into our upper torso. We feel our lungs filling up, expanding as the heh fills our upper torso. **Good.*** (Pause)

The long vav of the divine name is the oxygen path. We watch the oxygen flow all through our body, long like the vav of the Holy Name. Yud through the nostrils and head... Heh thru the torso, chest, arms. Vav through the length of our bodies, down to the feet. (Pause)

Now the heh of the exhale. Follow the full exhale until we are empty. Stay just a moment with the emptiness.

Open to the yud, as we fill our nostrils with breath. Move smoothly to the heh, the upper torso - the vav, the oxygen path - and the final heh of the exhale. We'll continue to watch our breath as we envision the divine name giving us life. We each breathe at our own pace. (Pause) If our mind wanders, we gently return to our breath. We will continue for several moments.

ENERGY TIP: Close this section with a familiar and easy chant, letting the volume build as participants reconnect with the group energy.

MODEH ANI: BLESS THIS DAY GUIDED MEDITATION
FOR ALL AGES

Gratefulness is a basic religious attitude. The prophet Isaiah named God as the One who creates good and evil, darkness and light (Is. 45:7). The practice of blessing God for both the good and the "challenges" is a deeply comforting dimension of the Jewish way.

This guided meditation can stand as an exercise or as a preparation for the Modeh Ani section of the service.

> *LEADER: As we prepare to recite Modeh Ani, we want to imagine the day ahead of us. We want to see the best possible outcome for all the situations and all the interactions of the day ahead.*

Use one of the relaxation techniques. Continue.

> *Let's close our eyes. Feel where we are right now. We want to sit comfortably, centered and relaxed. In our mind's eye, move forward from this moment and look ahead into the experiences of this day.*
>
> *Where will you spend this morning?* (Pause)
>
> *Who will you see today?* (Pause) *What will you do? How do you feel about this? Sense and visualize a joy accompanying you this morning. Imagine the best possible outcome for all the experiences of the day. Continue to visualize your day, blessing all the experiences that lie ahead.* (Pause)
>
> *If you come to a moment that you expect will be difficult or unpleasant, stop there. Stay with that scene. What is your best hope for that moment? What do you hope to say or do or feel?*

What do you hope that other people will experience? What practical steps can you take to prepare for this outcome? Each time you foresee a challenging moment, imagine that everyone involved in this encounter is guided by their best intentions. Thank God for the insight and strength you will need to meet this challenge.

Continue looking at all the moments of the day ahead. Envision the qualities you want to see in each moment: understanding, fullness, love. Fill each moment with blessing and gratitude.

ENERGY TIP: Close the experience, by softly singing a familiar version of Modeh Ani. Build the volume as the group comes out of their private experience.

MODEH ANI
DISCUSSION GUIDE
FOR ALL AGES

The first prayer we say each morning confronts us with a theological challenge. In the Modeh Ani prayer, we say that we are grateful, but we may in fact be suffering in any number of ways! There is really no easy answer to this question; but our tradition has given us a number of possible approaches. This discussion guide allows students to begin to "reframe" our problems as challenges.

Leader opens the discussion:

> *What was your first thought waking up this morning?*
> *Did anyone wake up bright and perky? Why?*
> *Did anyone wake up in the doldrums? Why?*
> *(Spend some time with the group deciding how the first thoughts of the morning can effect the day and visa versa.)*
>
> *Can you pick how you feel?* (Elicit a few yeses and nos.)
> Hopefully the students will come up with this. If not, you raise it:
> *Have you ever anxiously anticipated something that turned out to be really okay? Have you ever had a difficult experience that turned out to be an opportunity?*
>
> *So we may not be in such a great mood when we wake up, yet our tradition asks us to begin each day with saying that we are grateful!*
>
> *When we say Modeh Ani, we can*
> *A: Really be in a good mood, or*
> *B: We can just mumble the words, or*
> *C: We can lie to God or*
> *D: We can remember that even if we are NOT looking forward to*

something that day, we are open to the idea that it can also be fine or even be an opportunity.

Discuss the pluses and minuses of these options.

Let's see if we can actually chose our feeling. Think of a time that you felt grateful for something. It could be something relatively small or inconsequential, like a hair cut working out well. Or it could be something more weighty, something like we have been discussing, when a hard situation worked out well. (Optional sharing. Make sure your examples are appropriate to the age and experience of your group) *So concentrate on this good experience. Concentrate on the feeling of gratitude. Imagine that the universe has bestowed this gift on you, this guiding hand, this help on your way. Silently in your heart, thank the universe for taking care of you in this way. Even if the prompt was something small, the feeling is real. You feel grateful and taken care of. You're fine. Thank the universe for this gift. . .*

Begin to sing Modeh Ani, until group catches on and sings with you. Sing for a while, slow it down. Sit quietly for a moment. Ask for feedback.

How do you feel now? Different than before the exercise?
You have homework: For the next week notice your first thought, do a little mental review of your upcoming day and use this song or meditation to "pre-bless" the day, especially the bumpy moments ahead!

TALLIT AS A ROBE OF LIGHT
GUIDED MEDITATION
FOR ALL AGES

This is a very short and simple meditation.

LEADER: *As we wrap up in our tallitot, we visualize the tallit as pure light. Hold it over your head and feel the light pour down through your body. Visualize the light shining down and slowly filling your body. Starting from our heads, (pause) feel the light cover and fill our heads (Pause after naming each body section), our shoulders, torsos, legs, our whole body, right down to our feet. We visualize ourselves filled with light. Feel this light filling us, surrounding us in our tallit-tent. We continue to sense this special light as we drape the tallit over our shoulders, and begin our davenning.*

Tallit as Blankie
For all ages

This lesson teaches the use of tallit as a way of connecting with nurturing aspects of God and our beautiful earth.

Begin by brainstorming with the group ways in which they feel supported and nurtured in their lives. Draw their attention in some detail to the incredible and complex systems that we need for virtually each moment of life. These might include:

- an atmosphere that protects us from dangerous radiation while letting in the warmth and light of the sun;
- a sky that rains down fresh water to nourish all life;
- all the micro-organisms in the soil that recycle the nutrients so that plants can grow to nourish and protect us;
- all the rest of life on earth, every species which plays some role in maintaining our life support system on the planet.

Take out a tallit or two and have the group members hold them and reflect on when they've seen tallitot. Have they seen people put them on by completely wrapping in them? Why would we put on clothing this way?

Many children have a blankie, an object that reminds them of the feeling of being comforted and protected. The tallit can work as a kind of blankie for adults. It reminds us of the aspects of the natural world that protect and nourish us. Tallit is a trigger mitzvah: Doing this mitzvah reminds us of all the other 612! Likewise in our metaphor, tallit is a trigger that reminds us that we are embraced by God.

Take a moment when you put on tallit as a group to call to mind that feeling of comfort and love as a private meditation under the tallit.

The Tallit as Divine Protection
For all ages

Leader: *In a complete siddur, there is a meditation before putting on the tallit that includes the following: Through the commandment of tzitzit, may my nefesh, ruach and neshama* (Three layers of soul; see Four worlds lesson plan on page 179) *and prayer be rescued from the chitzonim/external negative forces. May the tallit spread over them* (the aspects of my soul) *and save them, like an eagle rousing its nest, fluttering over her fledglings.*

Discussion: In the first part of the exercise, we spend some time identifying our chitzonim/outer distracting influences. What are the outer factors in our lives that pull us off center, away from how we hope to manifest?

Leader: *We are going to use the tallit as a reminder of those eagle wings that surround and flutter and protect the precious nest.* (Teach the bracha; put on a CD of eagles crying) *Recite your bracha and wrap yourself in your tallit. Visualize the tallit as an eagle, fluttering over our heads and driving away all the chitzoniim. Let the tallit hold you and protect you. Let every negative idea fall away.*

Discussion Method

Sit quietly in your tallit for a while. Draw the group back together to share the imagery or sensations they experienced. OR

Drawing Method

Create or decorate (with fabric markers) tallitot using the imagery of eagles or wings. Decorations can be large or as simple and small, as the student desires.

Ratzon Meditation
For teens and adults

*R*atzon, will or desire, is a fascinating Hebrew word. The same four letters can be rearranged to make the words: *Notzar*, to create and *Tzinor*, a channel or pipe. Together, the three arrangements of the letters translate into the idea: "Our desire creates a channel," or "Our willingness creates the opportunity."

רצון נוצר צנור

Channel   Creates   Will

When we recite the Ashrei prayer, we have the custom of touching the tefilin shel yad as we say You open Your hand... . We touch the *tefilin shel rosh* as we say "You provide each living thing with its desire/ratzon." The place of the *tefilin shel rosh* is the place of *Ratzon*. This place, the space just above the front of the head is the place where our will and God's will can meet. We pray and learn throughout our tradition that we desire to make God's will into our own will, that God fulfills the desire of those who are aligned with the divine will.

The space above and around our heads can be seen as a metaphor for the point of contact between humans and God. This is the place where a queen places her crown, where a Jew places *tefilin*, where the light filled Moses after his encounters with God overflowed, creating an aura that radiated around his head. One mystical teaching says the letter yud symbolizes this place. Yud is the beginning of each letter; the single point of the yud is written each time every Hebrew letter is drawn! Similarly, God can be imagined as the tiny spiritual point from which we draw our physical being.

This exercise draws our attention to this powerful physical place. After a quieting meditation, we will draw to mind some of the symbols associated with this seat of Ratzon. This exercise can be strengthened by using it in combination with donning tefilin, but tefilin are not required.

Share with the group any of the ideas from the introductory paragraph that will help them understand the concept of ratzon. If tefilin will be used, put them on now.

> **LEADER:** *Today, we are going to open ourselves to the Divine will. We will quietly concentrate on this part of ourselves, which*

the tradition teaches us is our antenna to God. Nothing else is required. We will simply concentrate on this special space.

Let's begin. Sit comfortably, with your eyes closed. With your mind's eye, watch the flow of breath through your body. From your head, through your torso, down your spine, legs. Up again and out with your exhale. Breathe slowly and fully, watching each breath with your mind's eye. (Pause)

Now move your attention to a space just above the top of your forehead, to the place of tefilin shel rosh. Hold your attention on that space above and between your eyes, as you continue to breathe fully and slowly. Feel the openness of that space. That point is your point of contact with eternity. The point of ratzon is shaped like the letter yud. The top of the yud is rooted in the Divine mind and the bottom of the yud touches your mind. Imagine the yud. Sense that you are following the yud up, up and up to your Creator, to your potential, to your purpose. Feel the fullness, the expansiveness, of your root in the Divine. Now follow the yud, all along that channel, that root, right back to you. Feel the point where the yud touches your skin, your self. (Pause) *Now see both ends of the yud: The yud in its highest reaches and the yud as it touches you. Feel yourself expanding. You are opening to your root in the divine.* (Pause). *Sit quietly now. Allow the energy to flow back and forth along the path of the yud.*

Now watch as the yud enters your mind. The top of the yud comes down, down. The yud is contained in your mind. Sit quietly for just a moment more. Absorb any wisdom that is coming to you today from this higher source. Quietly take a moment to integrate this new information, this higher perspective. When you feel ready, slowly open your eyes....

Kavanot for Wearing the Tefilin

When we put on tefilin, we are essentially binding ourselves - committing ourselves - to do God's work. What is it that deserves and needs all the strength (arm), feeling (heart) and consciousness (headpiece) you can give? This could be a life-long value or goal. It could be a special task which you have in your near future. We will refer to this goal at each step of binding our tefilin this morning.[5]

> **AS YOU PLACE THE TEFILIN ON YOUR ARM:** *Connect your heart and strength to the goal. Say the first blessing aloud:*
>
> בָּרוּךְ אַתָּה ה' אֱלֹהֵינוּ מֶלֶךְ הָעוֹלָם אֲשֶׁר
> קִדְּשָׁנוּ בְּמִצְוֹתָיו וְצִוָּנוּ לְהָנִיחַ תְּפִילִין
>
> **ON THE FIRST WIND:** *I give my expansive power to this worthy goal;*
>
> SECOND: *I commit myself to the hard work it will take;*
>
> **THIRD:** *The beauty of this goal is worthy of my motivation and commitment;*
>
> FOURTH: *However long it takes, I am committed;*
>
> FIFTH: *Each moment and each step partakes of the end goal;*
>
> SIXTH: *This goal is so important that it is becoming part of me.*
>
> SEVENTH: *This goal is so much a part of me that I am helping to make it real in the world.*

---

[5]This seven part Kavanah is based on the sefirotic system. See page 47 for a diagram.

PUT ON THE HEADPIECE: The front covers the third eye of intuition, the back connects with the base of the skull, where ideas develop into motivation and action. Again, "refocus" as you adjust your headpiece. Say the second blessing:

בָּרוּךְ אַתָּה ה' אֱלֹהֵינוּ מֶלֶךְ הָעוֹלָם אֲשֶׁר קִדְּשָׁנוּ בְּמִצְוֹתָיו וְצִוָּנוּ עַל מִצְוַת תְּפִילִין

As you say "Baruch atah ha'Shem..." straighten out the straps of your Tefilin by holding on to where they begin, at the knot at the nape of the neck. Follow the straps down the length of your body and set them over your thighs. You are "bringing your intention down" into the world of action.

AS YOU WRITE GOD'S NAME ON YOUR HAND: You complete your act of devotion: May God's name be visible in the work of your hands.

Kavanot for Wearing the Tefilin

An alternative meditation has each of the seven circles of tefilin on the arm match up with one word from the line on the Ashrei prayer, which refers to the power of God's extended hand:

Poteach	Open	פּוֹתֵחַ
Et	the Fullness	אֶת
Yadecha	of Your hand	יָדֶיךָ
U masbia	and provide	וּמַשְׂבִּיעַ
L'chol	every and all	לְכָל
Chai	living beings	חַי
Ratzon	with its needs	רָצוֹן

These exercises involve a hefsek, an interruption between reciting the blessing on a mitzvah and executing its performance. (See note on page 26). Some may prefer to use these kavanot only in a teaching setting, or to say the words inaudibly.

Ten Spheres of Nothingness - Thirty two Paths of Wisdom

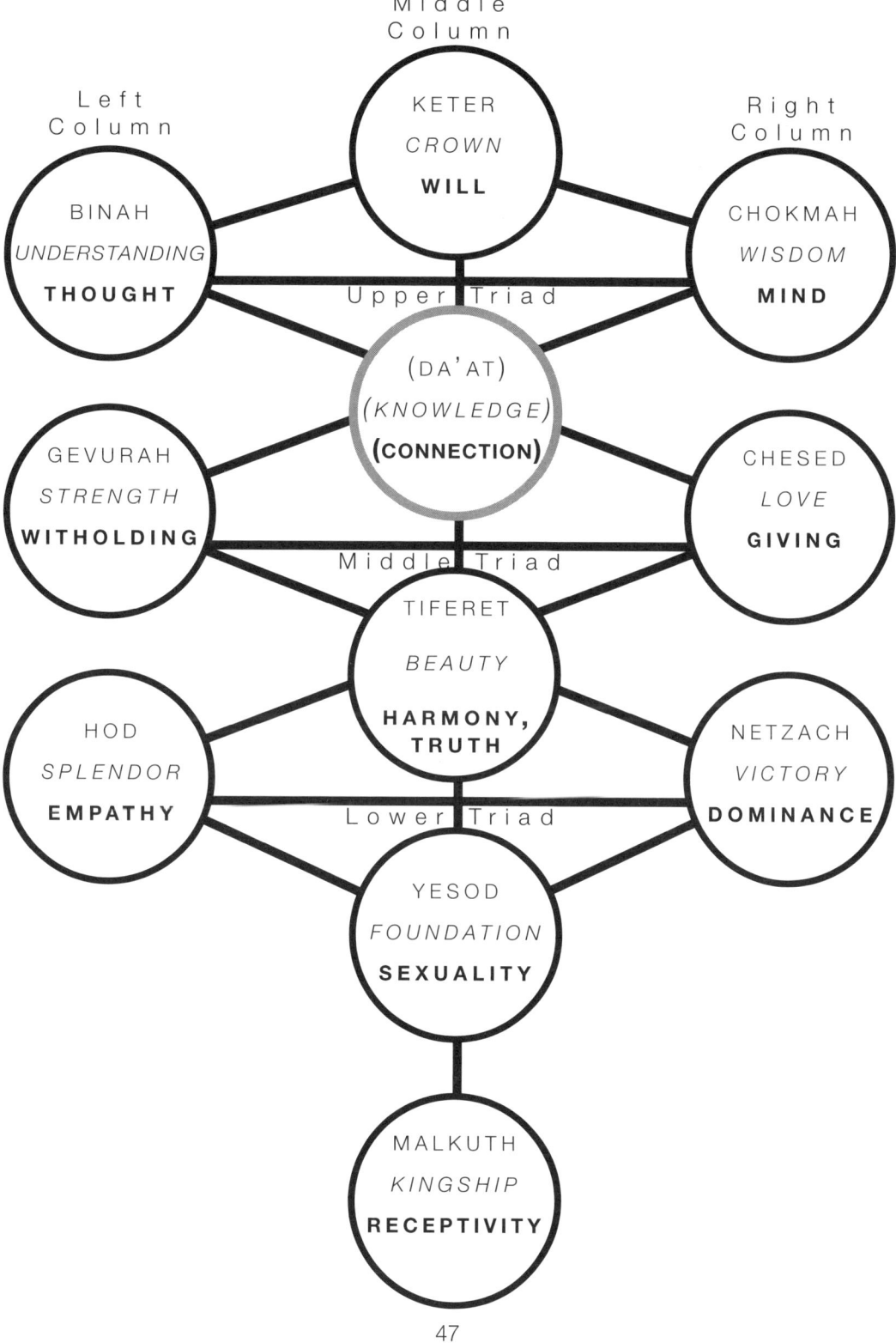

Mah Tovu Section
For all ages

The Mah Tovu prayer names many of the sacred spaces of the Jewish people from the tents of our ancestors to the elaborate First and Second Temples. This prayer opens the worship service because we make our surroundings into a place of awareness and holiness when we pray.

These exercises are concrete ways of helping students experience the transition into a prayerful environment.

The Tallit Dance

Hold a large tallit over a central space in the room. Begin humming "Mah Tovu" and invite people to walk slowly into the davenning space, as they feel ready. Sing "Mah Tovu" once or twice again when everyone is included under the tallit.

Or, spend a few minutes describing the imagery of the tallit (wings, Shechinah, God's presence, the cloud that led the Israelites in the wilderness). Ask the group to close their eyes. With another tall person, spread a tallit over the group andgently wave the tallit over the group, so the children can feel a soft breeze, the wings of the Shechina passing over them. Hum or sing "Mah Tovu."

The Bridge

Have two people create a bridge with their arms held overhead (as in London Bridge children's song) Begin singing "Mah Tovu." One by one, people enter under the bridge and add their voices to the song, and create a circle on the other side of the bridge. When everyone has gone under, the bridge people join the circle. Sing the song together again.

Gathering Meditation

Jews create sacred space with architecture (for example, a synagogue or a huppah), with ritual objects (for example, tallit and candles) and with our intentionality (by prayers or kavanot). The Mah Tovu prayer, which initiates the morning service, mentions a series of spaces that have been sacred for our people: the tents of our ancestors and our Temples. In this meditation, we will practice the emotional work of creating personal sacred space.

Leader: *In the Mah Tovu prayer, we enter prayer space, holy space. We recall the tents of our ancestors: Abraham's tent was open on all four sides so he could greet and comfort any wanderer. We remember Sarah's tent was filled with light all the days of her life. We recall the tents of Jacob, the humble and modest and beautiful tents described by the prophet Bilam.*

Mah Tovu Section

So go into your tent today. If you have a tallit, you can cover yourself with it and really enter your own tent. Let's close our eyes now and begin to gather ourselves into this holy space. Feel the tent of your body. Notice your breath, be aware of your physical body.

Now expand the focus of your attention and notice the space around you (Pause)

Feel the special quality of the space you are creating with your attention. Feel welcome in this space. (Pause)

Notice if there are any parts of you that do not feel so welcome in this space. Make a small circling motion with your arms and invite these parts of yourself into the tent. Be with them in this loving space. (Pause)

Now open your tent to include the people we are with today. Notice if any of them do not feel comfortable in this space with you. Make a small gathering motion with your arms, as if you are drawing something close to your heart. Invite these individuals into this loving space with you. Be with them now. (Pause)

Open your tent now to the people in your life, in your work and home, in your class and your community. Share with them the light and love you feel now. If there are any who are slow or shy to enter this space, make a small gathering motion with your arms and invite them in now. Each and every one of us is together in this tent.

(To conclude, move into singing a familiar tune for Mah Tovu.)
To move out of the meditation, say:

We have filled the space around us with a loving and prayerful energy. Return to an awareness of THIS room, but stay in your tent. Keep that energy present, as we continue the service on...

Birchot Ha-torah Teaching & Learning Experience
For all ages

We accept the Torah each day with the recitation of the Birkhot HaTorah, part of the morning service. Following the blessings, small portions are read from Torah, Mishnah and Gemara. In this exercise, each participant has the experience of receiving and giving a Torah insight that has special meaning for him or her.

Break your group up into groups of 3 or 4 people. Distribute the Torah insights sheets on the attached page.

> **Leader:** *There is a midrash that teaches that Torah is being given at Mt Sinai, all the time, right now. God is constantly giving over laws and insights. And we accept Torah every day by studying it and practicing it. Every morning, we thank God for the gift of Torah in the early part of the morning service. Today we are going to receive and give Torah.* **(Distribute verses)**

Scan the teachings on the handout. Find the one that has the strongest message for you today. Think about the message. Why does it have special meaning for you? Read the message to the people in your group and explain to them why it is special for you today.

Adjust the Torah Ideas for your group. You may use the Torah ideas to review ideas from other lessons you are learning with your class. You can select verses that introduce new subject areas, and so on.

Torah Insights

1. The entire world is just a narrow bridge and the main goal is to never be afraid. (Rebbe Nachman of Bratlav)

2. It is a very great mitzvah to be in a constant state of happiness. (Rebbe Nachman of Brastlav)

3. When the children of Israel received Torah, they were as one person with one heart. (Rashi on Exodus 19:2)

4. Jerusalem lies in ruins because we were not mindful of the Oneness of God, morning and night. (BT Shabbat 119b)

5. Whatever is hateful to you, do not behave that way towards another. (Pirke Avot)

6. A person must praise God when difficult things occur, as well as when he enjoys good fortune. (BT Berachot 56B)

7. There is no person who doesn't have his or her moment, no thing that doesn't have its place. Everything that God made is appropriate in its season. (Pirke Avot 4:3)

8. God loves a person who does not display his or her anger. (BT Pesachim 113:)

9. Hillel once observed a skull floating on the surface of a stream. He said to it: "Even though they drowned you because you yourself drowned another, they who drowned you will themselves be drowned." (Pirke Avot 2:7)

10. If a man's heart is heavy with worry, let him unburden himself to a friend. (Yoma 75.)

11. It is better to own less goods but to have peace of mind than to have more possessions with a tormented spirit. (Ecclesiastes 4:6)

12. The question most feared by the great Hasid Reb Zusya was not "Why weren't you more like our teacher Moses?" The question most feared by Reb Zusya was "Why weren't you more like Reb Zusya?"

Elohai Neshama* - A Chant
For older elementary through adult
*The tune by Rabbi Shefa Gold is included on the accompanying tape.

אֱלֹהַי נְשָׁמָה שֶׁנָּתַתָּ בִּי טְהוֹרָה הִיא:

This important morning blessing calls our attention to our breathing. Several words in the blessing contain hey hamapik; dotted heh s which are pronounced as deep exhales! This chant, on the accompanying tape is offered as a sample of the chanting technique. This particular chant makes a nice introduction to a quiet breathing meditation.

The leader teaches the song (see tips for teaching songs and chants, page 23). Simple percussion instruments can be used. Practice the song a few times and give some kavanah/intentional orientation for the song.

Sample Kavanot

> *<u>Elohai</u>, the name for God in this prayer is in the first person singular: My God - this deeply personal expression calls us to our own relationship with Ha-kadosh Baruch Hu. OR*
>
> *<u>Neshamah</u> means breath and also spirit. Each breath renews us. This is true, physically! Each breath is a cleansing of the blood stream. So too spiritually! Each deep breath can be a moment of renewal, of beginning again. OR*
>
> *<u>Tehorah</u> means pure or acceptable or clear. Ritual offerings needed to be in this condition, tahor. With this song, we become clear and worthy of being nearer to God.*

Share the kavanah with the group and begin a purposeful singing of the chant. As the chant leader, you need to put your attention in two places. The first and best thing you can do to strengthen a group's kavanah is to deepen your own kavanah! Any distracting thoughts that come to you are simply noticed and released. As the leader "How am I doing? Are people engaged in this?" is a common distracting thought.

On the other hand, as the leader, your attention does need to be with the group. Listen carefully for signs of insecurity. Does the song need to move a little faster or slow down a bit? You may need to remind people to blend their voices or listen to each other for the tempo. Sing together until the group sounds confident; and then sing a little more. The "little more" is the time when the repetition and the confidence and the beauty sets in. Slowly lower the volume or slow the speed to indicate to the group that the chant is ending. Remind them to breath quietly and fully for a few moments to enjoy the impact of the song.

THE MORNING WILL UNFOLD FOR US* AN ALTERNATIVE BIRCHOT HA-SHACHAR

FOR ALL AGES, ESPECIALLY YOUNG PEOPLE
*THE TUNE, BY RABBI SHEFA GOLD IS INCLUDED ON THE ACCOMPANYING TAPE.

This exercise is designed for children, pre-bar & bat mitzvah age. In a free-form fashion, it recalls most of the themes of a traditional birchot ha-shachar. L'shem chinuch (for the sake of learning) you may use it instead of birchot hashachar if your local custom allows.

This is a repeat-after-me song with hand and body movements. Approximate motions are fine. You may want your group to suggest new movements.

The morning will unfold for us (unfolding motion)
Life will rise from dust (scoop up with arms)
We're rising in remembrance (jump up on "rising")
Of your love. Hallelujah Hallelujah Hallelujah Hallelujah
(sway with arms open to receive the love, be seated)

You opened up our eyes to see (pop fingers open at eye level)
You have made us free (stretch open arms)
We're rising in remembrance (jump up on "rising")
Of your love. Hallelujah Hallelujah Hallelujah Hallelujah
(sway with arms open to receive the love, be seated)

You lift us up when we are down
(bend over, touch floor and slowly lift arms)
You share with us your royal crown (motion of crowning oneself)
We're rising in remembrance (jump up on "rising")
Of your love. Hallelujah Hallelujah Hallelujah Hallelujah
(sway with arms open to receive the love, be seated)

The Morning Will Unfold for Us
An Alternative Birchot Ha-shachar

You guide our steps at every turn
(hold hands with your palms together at chest level and snake your hands forward as if navigating twisty turns)
You teach us what we need to learn
(gather information with fingers, as if gathering sparks from the air around you and place them at your forehead)
We're rising in remembrance (jump up on "rising")
Of your love. Hallelujah Hallelujah Hallelujah Hallelujah
(sway with arms open to receive the love, be seated)

You give us strength when we are weak
(imitate early morning stretch)
Reminding us of what we seek
(put hand to brow and look around)
We're rising in remembrance (jump up on "rising")
Of your love. Hallelujah Hallelujah Hallelujah Hallelujah
(sway with arms open to receive the love, be seated)

Beyond imagination
(make a fist with the baby finger protruding, touch baby finger to forehead and draw little spirals into the air around your head)
Your presence fills creation
(arms out, palms up, sway, indicating God's bounty in creation)
We're rising in remembrance (jump up on "rising")
Of your love. Hallelujah Hallelujah Hallelujah Hallelujah
(sway with arms open to receive the love, be seated)

You lift the slumber from our eyes
(wipe eyes in exaggerated motion)
You signal for the sun to rise
(clap sharply and raise one hand from the platform of the second)

We're rising in remembrance (jump up on "rising")
Of your love. Hallelujah Hallelujah Hallelujah Hallelujah
(sway with arms open to receive the love, be seated) (2x)

Free Form Birchot Ha-shachar - Stylized Movement
For all ages

Most of the blessings of birchot ha-shachar take us through the normal morning routine of waking up, moving out of bed, dressing and so on. This version of birchot ha-shachar has us moving around, symbolically acting out these morning activities. After the group is familiar with the English phrases and the stylized movements, it is easy to introduce the Hebrew phrases back into the blessings.

Leader: *This morning we are going to act out the blessings that are part of the birchot ha-shachar. We'll say the beginning of each blessing in Hebrew with big movements. Let's stand in a circle. We need to be this far apart* (hold arms out). *Good. As we say* בָּרוּךְ אַתָּה *(Baruch atah) let's make a big deep bow and rise up as we say Adonai. Now, as we say* אֱלֹהֵינוּ מֶלֶךְ הָעוֹלָם *(Eloheynu melech ha-olam) God is God of the world, let's sway side to side in a big open movement. Good. Make it a real stretch. The birchot ha-shachar are the part of the morning service when we have just woken up. Let's get the blood flowing today.*

Let's try it again: Baruch atah Adonai, with a deep bow down and up; and Eloheynu melech ha-olam with a wide sway. Great.

Now, we can add the morning blessings. The first blessing is about the morning light. (Quote the translation you are using)

How can we show this? (Ask for some ideas. Embellish a little. For example, say "So you are showing the light emerging...").

Nice, let's try that one. Start with our Baruch movements and now add [insert name] version of "You gave the rooster the ability to tell day from night." Great.

Who has a motion for "You have made me a Jew"? How would you show "Jew"?

Continue devising stylized movements to each blessing.

> *ENERGY TIPS: If you use this formula as part of a prayer service, create a smooth transition to the next section of the service. You may want to chant something like, "You guide us back to our seats and page 57..."*

ברכות השחר
BIRCHOT HA-SHACHAR
ADULT/INTERPRETIVE VERSION

...You create in us the ability to distinguish light from night.
...You encourage me to wrestle with my faith
...You open me to new opportunities
...You pattern my form in Your image
...You inspire the visionless
...You wrap us in safety
...You free us from our prisons
...You move us beyond restricting limitations
...You ground us securely on this earth
...You provide for the multiplicity of my needs
...You guide our life's path
...You empower your people with strength
... You crown your people with dignity
...You re-energize the weary
...You awaken me to my potential.

בָּרוּךְ אַתָּה ה' אֱלֹהֵינוּ מֶלֶךְ הָעוֹלָם אֲשֶׁר נָתַן לַשֶּׂכְוִי בִינָה לְהַבְחִין בֵּין יוֹם וּבֵין לָיְלָה:

בָּרוּךְ אַתָּה ה' אֱלֹהֵינוּ מֶלֶךְ הָעוֹלָם שֶׁעָשַׂנִי יִשְׂרָאֵל:

בָּרוּךְ אַתָּה ה' אֱלֹהֵינוּ מֶלֶךְ הָעוֹלָם שֶׁעָשַׂנִי בֶּן (בַּת) חוֹרִין:

בָּרוּךְ אַתָּה ה' אֱלֹהֵינוּ מֶלֶךְ הָעוֹלָם שֶׁעָשַׂנִי בְּצַלְמוֹ:

בָּרוּךְ אַתָּה ה' אֱלֹהֵינוּ מֶלֶךְ הָעוֹלָם פּוֹקֵחַ עִוְרִים:

בָּרוּךְ אַתָּה ה' אֱלֹהֵינוּ מֶלֶךְ הָעוֹלָם מַלְבִּישׁ עֲרֻמִּים:

בָּרוּךְ אַתָּה ה' אֱלֹהֵינוּ מֶלֶךְ הָעוֹלָם מַתִּיר אֲסוּרִים:

בָּרוּךְ אַתָּה ה' אֱלֹהֵינוּ מֶלֶךְ הָעוֹלָם זוֹקֵף כְּפוּפִים:

בָּרוּךְ אַתָּה ה' אֱלֹהֵינוּ מֶלֶךְ הָעוֹלָם רוֹקַע הָאָרֶץ עַל הַמָּיִם:

בָּרוּךְ אַתָּה ה' אֱלֹהֵינוּ מֶלֶךְ הָעוֹלָם שֶׁעָשָׂה לִי כָּל צָרְכִּי:

בָּרוּךְ אַתָּה ה' אֱלֹהֵינוּ מֶלֶךְ הָעוֹלָם הַמֵּכִין מִצְעֲדֵי גָבֶר:

בָּרוּךְ אַתָּה ה' אֱלֹהֵינוּ מֶלֶךְ הָעוֹלָם אוֹזֵר יִשְׂרָאֵל בִּגְבוּרָה:

בָּרוּךְ אַתָּה ה' אֱלֹהֵינוּ מֶלֶךְ הָעוֹלָם עוֹטֵר יִשְׂרָאֵל בְּתִפְאָרָה:

בָּרוּךְ אַתָּה ה' אֱלֹהֵינוּ מֶלֶךְ הָעוֹלָם הַנּוֹתֵן לַיָּעֵף כֹּחַ:

בָּרוּךְ אַתָּה ה' אֱלֹהֵינוּ מֶלֶךְ הָעוֹלָם הַמַּעֲבִיר שֵׁנָה מֵעֵינַי וּתְנוּמָה מֵעַפְעַפָּי:

ברכות השחר
BIRCHOT HA-SHACHAR
YOUTH VERSION

...You gave the rooster the ability to tell day from night.
...You have made me a Jew.
...You have made me a free person.
...You have made me in Your image.
...You have given us the ability to see
...You have provided me with clothing and shelter.
...You help us grow beyond our limitations.
...You give us sure footing.
...You give us everything we need.
...You guide us on our path.
...You help us find the strength we need.
...You give us the crown of self-respect.
...You give us new strength each day.

בָּרוּךְ אַתָּה ה' אֱלֹהֵינוּ מֶלֶךְ הָעוֹלָם אֲשֶׁר נָתַן לַשֶּׂכְוִי בִינָה לְהַבְחִין בֵּין יוֹם וּבֵין לָיְלָה:

בָּרוּךְ אַתָּה ה' אֱלֹהֵינוּ מֶלֶךְ הָעוֹלָם שֶׁעָשַׂנִי יִשְׂרָאֵל:

בָּרוּךְ אַתָּה ה' אֱלֹהֵינוּ מֶלֶךְ הָעוֹלָם שֶׁעָשַׂנִי בֶּן (בַּת) חוֹרִין:

בָּרוּךְ אַתָּה ה' אֱלֹהֵינוּ מֶלֶךְ הָעוֹלָם שֶׁעָשַׂנִי בְּצַלְמוֹ:

בָּרוּךְ אַתָּה ה' אֱלֹהֵינוּ מֶלֶךְ הָעוֹלָם פּוֹקֵחַ עִוְרִים:

בָּרוּךְ אַתָּה ה' אֱלֹהֵינוּ מֶלֶךְ הָעוֹלָם מַלְבִּישׁ עֲרֻמִּים:

בָּרוּךְ אַתָּה ה' אֱלֹהֵינוּ מֶלֶךְ הָעוֹלָם מַתִּיר אֲסוּרִים:

בָּרוּךְ אַתָּה ה' אֱלֹהֵינוּ מֶלֶךְ הָעוֹלָם זוֹקֵף כְּפוּפִים:

בָּרוּךְ אַתָּה ה' אֱלֹהֵינוּ מֶלֶךְ הָעוֹלָם רוֹקַע הָאָרֶץ עַל הַמָּיִם:

בָּרוּךְ אַתָּה ה' אֱלֹהֵינוּ מֶלֶךְ הָעוֹלָם שֶׁעָשָׂה לִי כָּל צָרְכִּי:

בָּרוּךְ אַתָּה ה' אֱלֹהֵינוּ מֶלֶךְ הָעוֹלָם הַמֵּכִין מִצְעֲדֵי גָבֶר:

בָּרוּךְ אַתָּה ה' אֱלֹהֵינוּ מֶלֶךְ הָעוֹלָם אוֹזֵר יִשְׂרָאֵל בִּגְבוּרָה:

בָּרוּךְ אַתָּה ה' אֱלֹהֵינוּ מֶלֶךְ הָעוֹלָם עוֹטֵר יִשְׂרָאֵל בְּתִפְאָרָה:

בָּרוּךְ אַתָּה ה' אֱלֹהֵינוּ מֶלֶךְ הָעוֹלָם הַנּוֹתֵן לַיָּעֵף כֹּחַ:

בָּרוּךְ אַתָּה ה' אֱלֹהֵינוּ מֶלֶךְ הָעוֹלָם הַמַּעֲבִיר שֵׁנָה מֵעֵינַי וּתְנוּמָה מֵעַפְעַפָּי:

Pesukei D'zimrah

Cacophonous Davenning Exercise
For all ages

In a traditional prayer service, each individual recites much of the liturgy privately. The prayer leader will often begin a psalm or prayer by singing the first few lines. Congregants join in and hum or read the prayer in a unique balance of public and private experience. The prayer leader then recites the last few lines of the prayer aloud, thus keeping the group together.

This time of "humming along" is a wonderful opportunity to develop a strong personal "kavanah" or concentration. During these points in the worship, the whole congregation is quietly thinking about the same thing. The combination of group cohesion and personal devotion can support a deep experience of the prayer or psalm.

This exercise is a guide to teaching this "cacophonous" style of worship. The technique can be practiced in a classroom setting and incorporated into tefilot.

> **LEADER:** *Today we are going to practice a common davenning style called cacophony. Cacophony is a musical term. It means that many different sounds are heard at the same time. Often, in tefilot, we are all praying in our own way at our own pace. The cantor or leader keeps us together by saying the first few words and the last few words aloud. If the prayer leader goes a little too fast or if we don't really understand what we are saying, the style of prayer isn't as meaningful.*
>
> *We are going to really take our time today. You can say the prayer in English or in Hebrew. You might want to hum as you recite it. Use a tune that fits with the meaning of the words, happy or sad, major or minor, fast or slow.* (*If you as a leader/teacher are comfortable with music, you can encourage your students/ congregants to sing by demonstrating a few verses in the

traditional nusach/musical mode. You may even want to sing the instructions! This helps people get over some of the self-consciousness they may feel).

Look through the prayer below from the morning Pesukei D'zimra. Notice the images that are described, the beauty, and the enormous power. Close your eyes and see one of the images from this prayer. With your eyes closed, you may want to sway a bit, back and forth or side to side. Slowly. Slowly.

Now, we are going to pray this prayer, one line at a time. Keep your finger on the line you are reciting, so you can close your eyes between each line and come back to your place. Chant in Hebrew or the English, whichever has more meaning for you. Take your time, in silence or in music. I'll bring us all together at the end for the last phrase. (Begin humming and praying to start the group off.)

Tip: Choose a psalm from Pesukei D'zimrah which is rich in imagery or somewhat repetitive in structure. Ki l'olam chasdo is one example. Psalms 146 and 148 also work well with this exercise.

Baruch She-amar*
Chant & Sign Language
For older elementary through adult
*The tune by Rabbi Shefa Gold is included on the accompanying tape.

בָּרוּךְ הוּא בָּרוּךְ שְׁמוֹ בָּרוּךְ שֶׁאָמַר וְהָיָה הָעוֹלָם

Baruch she-amar is the opening song of the second section of the morning davenning, Pesukei D'zimrah, literally verses of praise. The full version of this prayer is an ever-building list of God's mercy and strength. One has the feeling that we small humans are so overwhelmed with God's presence that it's all we can do to sing back our praises! In this lovely tune, Rabbi Shefa Gold has caught the updraft in the intent of this prayer.

> **Leader:** *We are going to sing Baruch She-amar today as a three-part chant. In this chant, we are recognizing the enormous power that sustains all of creation. That power flows down to us. As we see it and feel it, we sing right back to the Source of All. In this chant, we recognize and bless the source of our blessings.*
>
> *The first part is simple and strong. This is the song of the earth catching the sustaining life-pulse of creation. It sounds like a heartbeat.* (Sing several times, adjust pronunciation and "heartbeat" beat-like sound)

בָּרוּךְ הוּא בָּרוּךְ שְׁמוֹ

> *The second part has the same words, but the tune rises more. This is the sound of the natural systems singing back to God. This is the song of rivers and clouds, of ostriches and mountains, of hamsters and breezes.* (Teach second part; optional discussion Who are you singing for today? Remind people to use their voice to give creation a way to sing)

בָּרוּךְ הוּא בָּרוּךְ שְׁמוֹ

Baruch She-amar* Chant & Sign Language

The third part is the human voice. This is more complicated, of course. There are more words. We sing Blessed is the One whose speech gives rise to all creation. We use our speech to sing back to that One. There is mutuality in this song. The tune rises and falls, like our own consciousness that rises and falls so much. (Teach the third part)

בָּרוּךְ שֶׁאָמַר וְהָיָה הָעוֹלָם

After we sing, we will sit quietly for a few moments. In that quiet time after our song, you can feel the energy of our song. Sit quietly with the mood created by our song.

Chanting Instruction: Start each part, in order. Adjust the kavanah, pace or any aspect that will help the group sing confidently. Sing for a few moments. Enjoy the sound and the feel of the group experience. Quiet the song by slowing or lowering your voice. Sit quietly for a few moments. Perhaps use a sentence or two to remind the group of the goal of the silence. Something like: **Let us add our silent intention this morning to the beautiful chorus we have just created.**

American Sign Language Instructions

Baruch: "Blessed;" begins with both hands shaped in a fist with the thumbs sticking up. Rest your thumbs lightly near your mouth and move them down and away in a flowing motion. The idea is to show that our words of blessing expand and move into the world.

Hu: "Him;" The right index finger points upward.

Sh'mo: "His Name;" is composed of two signs. First "Name;" Extend the index and middle finger of both hands and tuck the other fingers away. Cross your extended fingers, right over left, making an "X." The sign for "His" is the same as "Him," above.

BARUCH SHE-AMAR* CHANT & SIGN LANGUAGE

SHE-AMAR: "The One who spoke…" God "spoke" the world into being. The sign for "speak" begins by touching your pointed index finger to your lips. Draw a spiral in the air out in front of you, indicating words flowing from the mouth.

V': Hebrew prefix for "and." It is made by a small grasping motion of the right hand, in front of you at chest level, as if trying to lightly pull something along.

HAYA: This beautiful sign means "comes into being." Hold both hands open in front of you, palms up, at chest level. Circle your hands in flowing outward motions as if you are demonstrating the unfolding of creation.

HA-OLAM is Hebrew for "the world;" Make the letter "W" by extending the index through ring fingers on both hands and tucking away the pinkie and thumb. Circle your "W"s around each other as if they are two planets spinning around each other.

To utilize this exercise in a traditional service, simply continue to recite the Baruch she-amar prayer in the normal style.

Elohai Sacred Dance and Chant*

FOR ALL AGES
*THE SONG, BY LATIFA BERRY KROPF, IS INCLUDED ON THE ACCOMPANYING TAPE.

This lovely dance can be used to enhance group cohesion and a sense of invoking God's Presence. Following are instructions for all sacred dances.

1. The dance is a form of worship and should be done in an atmosphere of sacredness.
2. All the dancers work together to create kavanah.
3. The concentration is on blending voice, movement, and intention.
4. When the whole circle of dancers is holding hands, they are held with the left palm up and the right palm down.
5. Each dance is repeated many times at the discretion of the leader, so that the sound and movement can penetrate the dancers and the atmosphere.
6. Each dance ends with a silence during which time the dancers feel the energy of the dance in their bodies. Envision the energy radiating out through your heart to the world around you or down through your legs, deepening your roots in the ground.
7. The leader ends the silence by saying "Amen."
8. During partner dances, partners should be encouraged to make eye contact.
9. If the dance is being done incorrectly, they should be stopped, re-taught and begun again.

INSTRUCTIONS FOR ELOHAI DANCE:

Learn the song together and sing it until everyone feels confident singing.

Form one large circle and hold hands with the left palm up and the right palm down. Face slightly towards the left. The first time "Elohai" is sung, everyone takes four steps towards the left, while facing left. For the second "Elohai," everyone makes a partial turn towards the right, so people are almost walking backwards as they continue to circle to the left. For the third "Elohai" everyone faces forward and takes four steps in towards the center of the circle, raising up their hands together as they approach the middle. And during the fourth "Elohai," people take four steps back to the original circle and begin again.

> *ENERGY TIP: Repeat the dance and re-instruct as necessary. Continue the dance until you sense that each individual is experiencing the words and motions as they are executed. You can do one round in silence movement and then one in a strong voice for a touch of drama. Close the dance with a silence and an "Amen."*

The Illustrated Ashrei
For all ages

The Ashrei prayer is oft recited and its beautiful language is little understood. The goal of this activity is to teach some of the important terms of the Ashrei and to enhance the student's appreciation of its message.

Use the interpretive translation on the following page and discuss with the group.

Discuss ways in which these ideas can be interpreted. (Is it God's hands that open to feed all beings? What is the human role in that?) Move the class towards concrete images for each verse. Distribute art materials. (Murals, construction paper, fabric, whatever time, talent and space allow!) Illustrate the verses. Be sure to include the Hebrew verse in the artwork. Use the art to decorate davening space or common areas.

> *This exercise works very well with any prayer that has good imagery. Phrases from the Birkat Ha-mazon, Aleynu and Adon Olam are great candidates for illustration.*

An Interpretive Translation of Ashrei

א **Aleph:** People who feel close to God have a great happiness.
ב **Bet:** Every day gives me a new reason to feel blessed.
ג **Gimel:** The vastness of God's creation is mind-boggling.
ד **Dalet:** One generation teaches the other about the mystery of existence.
ה **Heh:** I notice the beauty of Your works and I want to talk about it!
ו **Vav:** I feel agitated by the wonder of it all. It helps me to express myself in words.
ז **Zayin:** Your fairness makes me happy
ח **Chet:** God puts up with our weaknesses and shortcomings
ט **Tet:** God's blessings nourish and sustain everything
י **Yod:** We sense what we receive from You, and we feel moved to give back.
כ **Kaf:** Your power is obvious throughout creation.
ל **Lamed:** We remind each other that it is Your power we see in creation.
מ **Mem:** Natural laws govern all space and all time.
ס **Samech:** God provides support for all of our weak moments.
ע **Ayin:** Every living thing relies on the Oneness for all its needs
פ **Peh:** God's open hand provides food for all.
צ **Tzade:** Things turn out fairly in the end
ק **Kuf:** God is present in every moment for those who seek.
ר **Resh:** God is a partner with people who are willing to do good work
ש **Shin:** People who work for the good feel God's protection and partnership.

THE SHEMA AND HER BLESSINGS

The Barchu prayer serves as a gathering of the community for the core of the prayer service. This song/dance explores the imagery of blessing (the word for "blessing" also means pool!) In the song, we dip into the pool of blessing. This exercise is appropriate for prayer settings in which there is no minyan. The traditional Barchu is only said in the presence of a minyan.

BARCHU, DEAR ONE*

FOR ALL AGES

*THE TUNE, BY HANNA TIFERET SIEGEL, IS INCLUDED ON THE ACCOMPANYING TAPE.

The leader sings each line with the hand motions, the group repeats. Leader faces group for instruction; the dance can be done in a circle or with the leader in front. The last lines are sung in unison. Repeat several times until the group can chant the prayer smoothly. This is a free-form dance; the participants can interpret the instructions in an open and flexible way.

> *Barchu   Dear One   Shechina   Holy Name*
> *When I call on the light of my soul, I come home*
>
> **Barchu** (2 x; leader then group; dip into a deep imaginary well in the center of the group)
> **Dear One** (2 x; sprinkle energy from that well on yourself)
> **Shechina** (2 x; raise hands up rapidly with the hands fluttering winglike)
> **Holy Name** (2 x; pull hands down in front of you, through your center, as if energy is pouring through you)
> **When I call on the light of my soul, I come home** (All together; put hands to mouth in a calling motion, reach out and step forward on "When I call on the light of my soul." Gather the energy into your heart and step back into your place for "I come home.")
>
> Repeat.

Yotzer Or: This Little Light of Mine*

FOR ALL AGES
*THE TUNE, AN AMERICAN GOSPEL CLASSIC, IS INCLUDED ON THE ACCOMPANYING TAPE.

This first blessing of "Shema and her blessings," (as the Talmud refers to this section) calls our attention to the quality of light. The morning Shema blesses the "creator of lights;" the evening Shema opens by blessing the One that makes "cycles of light and dark."

If you are helping a community or class build their understanding of the structure of the daily service, you might want to sing this song and then close with the appropriate chatimah/closing blessing. Have some fun with it; make harmonies and little gestures to act out the words.

> *Refrain*
> *This little light of mine, I'm gonna let it shine* (3x)
> *Let it shine, let it shine, let it shine.*
> *Verse*
> *I won't let anyone whoowh it out,* (make blowing motion, as if your finger is a candle and you are blowing it out)
> *I'm gonna let it shine* (3x)
> *Let it shine let it shine let it shine.*
>
> *Make up your own verses! For a camp setting, try:*
> *Feel the sun rise over the lake, I'm gonna let it shine...*
> *Or*
> *Friends and fun and feeling good, I'm gonna let it shine... etc.*

Create and add your own verses as appropriate to your class or community
---

THE KEDUSHAH DANCE*

FOR TEENS AND ADULTS

*THE TUNE, BY HANNAH TIFERET SEIGEL, IS INCLUDED ON THE ACCOMPANYING TAPE.

This song/dance can also be incorporated into the third paragraph of the Amidah or the Kedushah D'Yotzer. The Kedusha Dance requires a minimum group of around 20. It is most appropriate for teens and adults.

> **LEADER:** *Two of the greatest Prophets of Israel, Isaiah and Ezekiel had the experience of rising to heaven and hearing angels speak! These men reported the words that they heard the angels say and those words were embedded in our prayer book. We may not be angels or even prophets, but we say these words today so we can be as close to God as possible.*
>
> *The Siddur describes different kinds of angels with different jobs. Some of them are closer to God; some are closer to humanity. We are going to divide up today into three angelic camps. Each of you can pick which angelic camp that suits you best. In the center camp, we need the Serafim, the fiery angels. These are the most intense beings, the fireflies.*
>
> *The second circle will be the "Wow" angels, the Tzevaot, the Holy Hosts. We usually say that the Holy Hosts are like the stars, so you are the angels who say, "Wow, look at that, look at that grandeur."*
>
> *The third circle is the Chayot Ha-kodesh, the holy creatures, the grounded ones. You are the angels who are the most practical. The fiery angels stand closest to the holy light. They are the ones who can be touched by and transmit its powerful energy. Those who think of themselves as intense or risk takers should form this*

circle now. (Take a moment to adjust the circle and make it as circular as possible) *Your song is simple, you chant "Kadosh." What else can one say when facing this awesome power? Hold your hands up in front of you, palms to the center. Imagine the powerful clear light pouring through the middle of your small circle. Chant "Kadosh" as you modulate the light, receive it and change it into a form that can be passed on to the next circle of angels.*

Okay, the next group is the Wow angels, You are the really appreciative angels. Come in now and form your second circle around the fireflies. Face to your left, we are going to move slowly clockwise. We catch the energy emitted by the Serafim with our two hands reaching in towards them. Then we reach high up and out with our left hand as if watching the creation unfold in billions and billions of processes. Our singing part is "Yah tzevaot/God of multitudes."

Now for the Chayyot Ha-kodesh, the Holy grounded angels. Our job is to carry the life force coming down from Serafim and the Tzevaot and pass this energy on down to the earth. Then we gather up the prayers from the planet and send them back up the chain. This is a kind of spiritual recycling. So we face the center and slowly spin in a small circle, like a planet rotating on its axis; we move in a circle to spread that energy out into the world and gather in the prayers of humanity. We continue to circle (always to the left) and raise those prayers back up the angelic ladder. Our song is "me'lo kol ha-aretz k'vodo; The whole earth is full of God's splendor." (Take a moment to adjust the circle and make it as circular as possible)

The leader now starts the angelic choir, one group at a time, starting with the inner circle. Adjust motions so the groups are moving in a coordinated fashion. Make sure that people know their song well so they can meditate on the quality of the experience. You will get a feeling for when to slow the song down and quiet it. Slowly end the song. Instruct the groups to continue singing their part silently. Hold for a moment; don't be afraid of the silence.

> *If this exercise is used as part of a service, continue with your service. If you are using this as a classroom experience, create a transition back to your next activity. For example, you may want to thank everyone for being such good "angels" and that we intend to carry that loving feeling back into our life on earth.*

Ahavah Rabba and V'ahavta: A Drawing Exercise
FOR ELEMENTARY SCHOOL STUDENTS

Just before we recite the first line of the Shema, we chant the prayer called Ahavah Rabbah. This prayer talks about how God loves us. The very first line of the prayer makes this clear: "Ahavah Rabbah Ahavtanu," "With great love have You (God) loved us." Just after we recite the first line of the Shema, we chant the V'ahavta. This prayer talks about how we are to love God. The very first line of the prayer makes this clear: "V'ahavta et Adonai Elohecha," "You shall love Adonai Your God."

> **LEADER:** *There are many ways that God shows love to us, and many ways that we can show love to God. Let's take two pieces of paper. On the top of one of them, write* אַהֲבָה רַבָּה אֲהַבְתָּנוּ *(Ahavah rabbah ahavtanu). Underneath this, draw pictures of how you think God shows love to us in the world and in our lives. Then, take another piece of paper and on the top of it, write* וְאָהַבְתָּ אֵת ה' אֱלֹהֶיךָ *(V'ahavta et Adonai Elohecha). Underneath this, draw pictures of how you think we can show love to God in the world and in our lives.*

It would be a wonderful idea to decorate the place in which we play, or a classroom, or childrens' rooms at home with these pictures of God's love of us and of our love of God.

KAVANAH BEFORE THE SHEMA
FOR ALL AGES

This exercise should not be used during the service itself; it would require the worshipers to make a "hefsek/interruption" in a part of the service that should not be interrupted, according to halachah. Use the exercise outside of the worship service as a preparation for reciting the Shema. Once people are used to this idea, you may want to incorporate 5-10 seconds of silence immediately before the Shema is recited in the service itself. One of the relaxation techniques on pages 28-33 should be used first.

> **LEADER:** *Often, in a service in a Yeshivah Gevohah (a Yeshivah for adults), when the congregation reaches the Shema in the service, there is a pause of 5-10 seconds of silence before the chanting of the first line of the Shema. Then, the group does not recite the Shema in unison with a melody, as many congregations do. Rather each individual recites the first line of the Shema -- out loud -- at his own pace, in his own chant.*
>
> *During that pause before the Shema, we quiet our souls within us and we prepare ourselves to face God. We focus as consciously as we can upon the way we feel when God is closest to us. We kind of "wake ourselves up" to truly greet God. This prepares us to actually call upon God and to say: "Yes, I agree that "Adonai Elohaynu" as the Shema says; "Hashem is our God.".*
>
> *So, let's do that; let's say the Shema, but first let's pause to focus on God's presence. It is best to do this with our eyes closed for added concentration and to be ready to pray the Shema by heart. We begin... with a pause.*
>
> *During this pause, let's try to feel the way we do when we feel closest to God. Not asking God to do anything, not God asking*

us to do anything. Just the secure sense we have when God is near and loving; that is, how we feel when we realize God is close. We may have experienced this sense at night, perhaps, when we are afraid and lonely, or some other time when we needed God's comfort. We want to evoke that feeling now not out of any need: We don't want to ask anything of God. We just want to be close to God as part of our every morning and evening, as the Sages ordained.

So. Let's start now by saying no words, none of the words of the Shema yet. Cover your eyes with one hand as we traditionally do when we recite the Shema.

Take a deep breath slowly, and let it out slowly.
Recall now and feel the closeness of God... Stay with this feeling for 5-10 seconds.

Now, slowly, say or sing each word of the Shema slowly, at our own pace, realizing that as we say the words, we are welcoming God's presence to ourselves.

Guided Meditation on the 6 Corners of the Shema: God above, below and in the four directions*

For all ages

* This guided meditation is included on the accompanying tape

One of the obstacles we face in trying to say our prayers with kavanah/intention is the fast speed of many of our services. There is a tradition going back to the Talmud to slow things down, especially when reciting the Shema: "Rabbi Yirmiyah was sitting before Rabbi Chiyya bar Abba and saw that he took a long time in saying the Shema. Rabbi Yirmiyah said to him: 'As long as you have accepted God as Ruler above, below, and in the four directions, you do not have to do anything else.' (Berachot 13b).

Let's take some time to truly accept God's presence everywhere as we say the Shema.

As we recite the first line of the Shema, we visualize God's presence "above," in the heavens, among the stars and faraway worlds, as high as we can imagine, and "below" -- down here on earth -- north, south, east, and west of us. Let's try it:

> **Leader:** *With your eyes closed, imagine your head tilting upwards, and your eyes seeing the blue of the sky, and everywhere you look, and you feel: God is there. Imagine you can see beyond the blue of the sky, as if you were tracing the flight of a rocket as it leaves the Earth's atmosphere, and slowly it gets darker and darker, with a few pinpoints of light appearing -- planets and stars slowly emerge from the blackness. And you feel: God is here. Your vision is able to continue beyond our solar system through vast distances in space as you see bright galaxies, clusters of stars and gases of every color, and nebulae of immense shape. And you feel: God is here too.*

Now: We return our gaze to the Earth. Picture the planet Earth as the astronauts have seen it: a beautiful bright blue and white ball slowly spinning free. As you come closer to the Earth's surface, you see lakes and long rivers, waves of water that stretch over measureless oceans. You feel: God is here. Your mind's eye travels over mountains, hills, plateaus, and fields, and you feel: God is here. Colors of plant-life greet you: Lots of green, but also yellow, and purple and red and violet and blue and brown and every combination, in every shape; flowers, leaves, vines, trees. God is here.

There are animals of every kind in front of you: Walking, running, burrowing, sitting, lying. And there are people. In the mountains and fields, and in the villages and cities. People whose faces are of different shapes and sizes. Millions of people. And God is here.

We are part of all of it. Turn your attention now back to your body and all the sensations you are feeling right now. And God is here...

Slowly recite the first line of Shema Yisrael...

שְׁמַע יִשְׂרָאֵל ה' אֱלֹהֵינוּ ה' אֶחָד:

Return the group's attention back to their physical surroundings and move gently into the next activity.

Three Part Shema Round & Dance*

For all ages
The tune, by Lev Freidman, is included on the accompanying tape.

LEADER: *We are going to sing the Shema today as a dance, a three-part dance. Each part of the song is one way of expressing the idea of the Shema. Once you know all three parts, you can pick the message you like the best and sing/dance that one.*

The first part is really the inner message of the Shema, the complete Oneness of everything. The movement part looks like a little Aleph: We raise both hands up, touch both hands to our chest, open both hands down to either side of our thighs and back again to our chest. Do you see the Aleph we are making? The words are very simple: God is God. Adonai (up) Hu (at heart) Ha-elohim (down), Adonai Hu Ha-elohim. Here's the tune... (Practice together). **Good!**

ה׳ הוּא הָאֱלֹהִים

The second section is the Shema itself. We are going to dance this as a gathering, we want to gather all the world's people into the knowledge that we are all connected.

Hereís our gathering motion, reach out with your right and pull in towards your heart. Now reach out with the left hand and draw in towards your heart. Good. Here's the song... (Practice together). **Shema** (reach out with right hand) **Yisrael** (pull in towards heart) **Adonai** (reach out to left) **Eloheynu** (pull in towards heart) **Adonai** (out to right) **Echad** (in towards heart), **Adonai** (reach out to left) **Echad** (in towards heart).

Three Part Shema Round & Dance

שְׁמַע יִשְׂרָאֵל ה' אֱלֹהֵינוּ ה' אֶחָד:

The third part is the part for you if you are an outgoing type of person. The first part was a kind of quiet witnessing of God's unity, the second part is an invitation. The third part is like an advertisement. The motion is like broadcasting. Take your hands and sprinkle the message out there. Tell everyone.

Move from right to left and back again, sprinkling your message all around. Great! Now, here's the song for your part: Baruch shem kevod...

בָּרוּךְ שֵׁם כְּבוֹד מַלְכוּתוֹ לְעוֹלָם וָעֶד

ENERGY TIP: Each part is very simple, but putting them together is a little tricky. Stay in there and guide the groups so they are hearing each other and hearing how the sections fit together. This song is very energized. People will want to move around and sing it for a while. When you are done singing, give clear directions with your voice to slow and quiet the song down.

V'ahavta: A Sign-Language Exercise For elementary school students

Almost each word of the V'Ahavta has its own sign related to the meaning of the word. When students use these hand signals in prayer, it has the effect of "waking" them up: They are no longer simply sitting and reading or chanting. They are "embodying" the words.

I will only describe each symbol in words. This is stylized motion, not ASL; feel free to adjust the movements in a free and interpretive manner.

וְאָהַבְתָּ **V'AHAVTA** - Pat the top, left part of your chest over your heart three times, one for each syllable of the word V'ahavta.

אֵת ה' אֱלֹהֶיךָ **ET ADONAI ELOHECHA** - Make a large circle with your hand right in front of you as you say these words to symbolize that God can be found everywhere.

בְּכָל לְבָבְךָ **BECHOL LEVAVECHA** - Pat your chest over your heart twice as we say that we are to love God with all of our heart.

וּבְכָל נַפְשְׁךָ **UVECHOL NAFSHECHA** - Pat your the top middle part of your chest twice to symbolize loving God with all of our soul. (Why the top middle part of our chest to point to our soul? We cannot, of course, pinpoint a physical place in our bodies wherein our soul resides. However, there are some hints in our tradition that connect the word for soul with either our necks, or our breathing, hence our lungs, which are located in the top middle portion of our chest).

וּבְכָל מְאֹדֶךָ **UVECHOL ME'ODECHA** - Make two fists and hold them up at the sides of your body in the stance of champion showing off one's might as we say we should love God with all of our might.

וְהָיוּ הַדְּבָרִים הָאֵלֶּה **V'HAYU HADEVARIM HA'ELEH** - Make a fist except for index finger, and wag your finger in front of you up and down as if we are instructing someone about "these words."

אֲשֶׁר אָנֹכִי **ASHER ANOCHI** - Take that index finger and pat your chest as if we are saying "these words which I am commanding to you..."

V'ahavta: A Sign-Language Exercise
For elementary school students

מְצַוְּךָ הַיּוֹם **METZAVECHA HAYOM** - Point your index finger straight out in front of you as if you are teaching this to someone else (metzavecha).

עַל לְבָבֶךָ **AL LEVAVECHA** - Pat your heart with your open hand.

וְשִׁנַּנְתָּם לְבָנֶיךָ **VESHINANTAM LEVANECHA** - Make a fist except for index finger, and wag your finger in front of you up and down as we did at the words V'HAYU HADEVARIM HA'ELEH to show that we ought to teach these words to our children.

וְדִבַּרְתָּ בָּם **VEDIBARTA BAM** - "And you shall speak of them..." -- Symbolize a mouth speaking by holding one hand out in front of you and touch your thumb to the top four fingers several times.

בְּשִׁבְתְּךָ בְּבֵיתֶךָ **BESHIVTECHA BEVEITECHA** - Fold your arms and hold them up in front of your and then lay them onto your chest to symbolize sitting down.

וּבְלֶכְתְּךָ בַדֶּרֶךְ **U'VELECHTECHA VADERECH** - Hold your bent arms on either side of your body, make fists, and swing your arms to and fro, as if you are taking a walk, as it says, "as you walk by the way..."

וּבְשָׁכְבְּךָ **U'VESHOBECHA** - Pretend to go to sleep by laying one palm of your hands on the other, put your hands on one of your cheeks, and tilt your head to one side.

וּבְקוּמֶךָ **UVEKUMECHA** - Raise both arms as high as you can, on both sides of your body, as if your stretching after waking up.

וּקְשַׁרְתָּם לְאוֹת עַל יָדֶךָ **U'KESHARTAM L'OT AL YADECHA** - Pretend to wrap tefilin on your arm by wrapping an imaginary leather strap around and around your arm from your elbow down to your fingers.

וְהָיוּ לְטֹטָפֹת בֵּין עֵינֶיךָ **VEHAYU LETOTAFOT BEIN EINECHA** - Pretend to wrap tefilin on your head: Use two hands to wrap an imaginary strap from the back of your head to the front of your head.

וּכְתַבְתָּם **U'CHETAVTAM** - Write in the air with an imaginary pencil.

עַל מְזֻזוֹת בֵּיתֶךָ **AL MEZUZOT BEITECHA** - Point in the direction of the mezuzah on the door of the room you are in.

וּבִשְׁעָרֶיךָ **UVISHE'ARECHA** - Point in the direction of the "gates" or the entrance of the house or building you are in.

V'ahavta: A Sign-Language Exercise
For elementary school students

וְאָהַבְתָּ אֵת ה' אֱלֹהֶיךָ בְּכָל לְבָבְךָ וּבְכָל נַפְשְׁךָ וּבְכָל מְאֹדֶךָ:
וְהָיוּ הַדְּבָרִים הָאֵלֶּה אֲשֶׁר אָנֹכִי מְצַוְּךָ הַיּוֹם עַל לְבָבֶךָ:
וְשִׁנַּנְתָּם לְבָנֶיךָ וְדִבַּרְתָּ בָּם בְּשִׁבְתְּךָ בְּבֵיתֶךָ
וּבְלֶכְתְּךָ בַדֶּרֶךְ וּבְשָׁכְבְּךָ וּבְקוּמֶךָ:
וּקְשַׁרְתָּם לְאוֹת עַל יָדֶךָ וְהָיוּ לְטֹטָפֹת בֵּין עֵינֶיךָ:
וּכְתַבְתָּם עַל מְזוּזוֹת בֵּיתֶךָ וּבִשְׁעָרֶיךָ:

SHEMA IN A SUMMER CAMP OR OVERNIGHT SETTING
FOR ELEMENTARY SCHOOL STUDENTS

The sages were on to something special when they said we ought to say the Shema in the morning and in the evening. They were on to the connection between nature and God. Nature gets our attention because of a change, a transition, like the sky turning from blue to pink to orange to gray and finally to black, or vice versa. We are taken out of our normal routine and we see things from a different, larger point of view. And just maybe, we can be more open to the possibility of God's presence.

And so, when we say the Shema we try to be open to God's presence in nature. And when we notice the "normal" changes in nature, this is the time to focus on the words of the Shema, בְּשָׁכְבְּךָ וּבְקוּמֶךָ (beshochbecha uvekumecha) "when you lie down and when you wake up."

1. If possible, schedule a prayer service at dawn or at dusk. This may be easier in the winter months when the sun both rises later and sets earlier. Say the Shema very slowly, thinking about the rotation of the earth: the way it catches the light of the sun. Remember the path of the those rays of light which miss the earth and go travelling far away into the outer reaches of our solar system and into the Milky Way Galaxy and beyond. See if this helps to bring you to feel God's closeness.

2. Try to schedule a prayer service outside, even if it is not at dawn or dusk exactly, and be especially conscious of the earth and the heavens that God created when you get to the Shema, and the words בְּשָׁכְבְּךָ וּבְקוּמֶךָ (*beshochbecha uvekumecha*).

3. At the least, arrange a service at which the participants can be close to the windows and face outside throughout (This connects with a tradition that all synagogues ought to have windows to make it easier for worshippers to experience God in nature).

4. Use a globe and a light to show clearly what is happening between the earth and the sun when the time of Shema comes.

If Shema is the Answer, What is the question?
For elementary and middle school students

Distribute writing materials. Describe the Shema as the answer to a question and discuss what the question might be. Introduce the question you will work with today.

> **Leader:** *Let's imagine that the Shema is an answer to the question: What is the most important idea that you want everyone to know? If you could communicate one sentence to the entire world, what would it be?* (Give time for writing and optional sharing after each step)
>
> *Let's assume that everyone now knows this idea. How do you want them to feel about it?*
>
> *How will people go about remembering this idea? What are other ways you can suggest for people to review the idea and deepen their feeling about it? Give three or four different ways people could remember this Big Idea.*
>
> *How can people demonstrate that they have this idea in their minds and hearts? How will the awareness show in their lives?*
>
> (Be creative: T-shirts, jewelry, occupations, et al)

Use selected student works as a supplement to the recitation of the Shema.

DERECH EDUT: DRAWING/WRITING EXERCISE
FOR ALL AGES

In this exercise we explore how reciting the Shema can help us feel closer to God. It is an exercise of *edut* - testimony - where each of us shares our belief in God woith our neighbors.

The fifteenth century Siddur commentator Rabbi David Abudraham[6] says that one of the reasons we say the Shema out loud is because it is "derech edut/the way of testifying." We declare in public, as witnesses -- like in a courthouse. "It is as if," says Abudraham, "everyone says to his neighbor 'Shema!' 'Listen!' I believe that Adonai our God is the only One in His world." This is the reason, he says, that the last letter of the word Shema, an ayin, and the last letter of the word Echad, a dalet, are written in large letters in the Sefer Torah. Ayin dalet in Hebrew spells "witness." - עֵד

שְׁמַע יִשְׂרָאֵל ה' אֱלֹהֵינוּ ה' אֶחָד:

If possible, view the first line of the Shema -- Deuteronomy 6:4 -- in a Sefer Torah before this exercise.

This is an exercise of "edut," of giving testimony. It is an exercise of each of us sharing our belief in God with our neighbors.

> **LEADER:** *In a moment, each of you will write down the image of God that you have as you recite the Shema. We should try to feel the way we do when we feel closest to God. Not asking God anything, not God asking us to do anything. Just the secure sense we have when God is near and loving; that is, how we feel when we realize God is close. We may have experienced this sense at night, perhaps, when we are afraid and lonely, or some other time when we needed God's comfort. We want to evoke that feeling now not out*

---

[6] <u>Abudraham HaShalem</u> (Jerusalem: Usha Press, 1963), p.80, Rabbi Abudraham wrote one of the earliest Siddur commentaries we have.

Derech Edut: Drawing/Writing Exercise

of any need: We don't want to ask anything of God. We just want to be close to God as part of our every morning and evening, as the Sages ordained.

Distribute writing materials to each participant.

LEADER: *Describe your vision of God in words. We are not trying to write down what God "is;" we are writing what it feels like when we feel close to God. We cannot capture God's essence in words, but we want to represent one vision we have of God in order to give edut, testimony, and share with others so that each of us can be influenced to draw closer to God's presence in prayer.*[7]

Encourage the participants to share their testimony in pairs or among the whole group.

---

[7] Based, in part, upon Bruce Kadden and Barbara Binder Kadden, <u>Teaching Tefilah: Insights and Activities on Prayers</u> (Denver: A. R. E. Publishing, 1994) p.49, #7.

THE ONE: A SONG & DANCE*
*THE TUNE, BY RABBI DAVID ZASLOW, IS INCLUDED ON THE ACCOMPANYING TAPE.

This song is great fun and easy to do. It is a good way to create a strong group feeling. It works well as an introduction to the Shema or as a kind of group icebreaker.

> The One,
> Every single One,
> Each one joined and united to the One (repeat).
> Echad, (we are united)
> Yachid, (we are unique)
> U myuchad, (we are special)
> Echad, Yachid, U myuchad   אֶחָד יָחִיד וּמְיוּחָד

> **LEADER:** *The Oneness of God and the connection of all people is such a central message of Jewish tradition. This simple song is a fun way to dance out that message!*
>
> *There are two parts to the song. The English part goes like this:*
>
> **The One,**
>
> **Every single One,**
>
> **Each one joined and united to the One** (repeat).

(Make spontaneous comments, such as "No one is left out!" "We're all part of this!" and so on. You can spontaneously start the dance by holding onto someone's hand and then reaching out with your other hand for someone else. Slowly snake your way around the room this way)

> *Now for the Hebrew part.*
> *Echad, (we are united)*
> *Yachid, (we are unique)*
> *U myuchad, (we are special)*
> *Echad, Yachid, U myuchad*   אֶחָד יָחִיד וּמְיוּחָד

Repeat. When the group has this new part down, add the English part.

ENERGY TIP: Drums and other simple percussion instruments work well with this song.

Two Role-Playing Exercises on the First Line of the Shema

For elementary school children

One thing we tend to forget is that the origin of the Shema is not in the Siddur. It is in the Torah itself! (Deuteronomy, 6:4). The first person to say the words of the Shema was Moses, in the last days of his life, as he spoke to all of Israel. He wanted them to hear the important thing he was saying. That is why he started with the word "Shema," which means "hear." He wanted all of Israel to hear and to remember that there is only one God. He wanted all of Israel to hear and to remember that this God is our God, that the people of Israel and God have a very close and special relationship.

These two role-playing exercises can be done one after the other, or on two completely separate occasions:

Playing Moses

Let's do some acting. Let's pretend we were there when the Shema was first said. Let's take turns playing Moses, while the rest of us pretend to be the people of Israel listening to Moses. When Moses said the words of the Shema to the people, he must have said it loudly and with a lot of emotion. He knew that the people had come out of Egypt not too long ago and were not used to worshiping only one God. Perhaps he used his arms in a certain way to show the people how important his words were. Perhaps he pointed to the people. Each "Moses" can decide how to say these words. If it is a small enough group, everyone can take a turn at playing Moses.

If it is a large group, this role-playing session can be done on different days, giving several participants a chance to play Moses each day.

Two Role-Playing Exercises on the First Line of the Shema

Tell Your Neighbor

Another way to act this out is hinted at in a commentary by Rabbi David Abudraham.[8] "It is as if," says Abudraham, "everyone says to his neighbor 'Shema!' 'Listen!' I believe that Adonai our God is the only One in His world!" According to this, each time we daven the Shema, everyone is playing Moses, and everyone is playing Israel too. We all ask all of us to listen as we declare that we believe there is only one God in the world.

> **LEADER:** *So, let's act this out. I want to ask all of us to stand up. Now, let's have the half of the group that is standing towards the front of the room turn around and face the people standing towards the back of the room. We are each going to say the Shema to each other. We are each going to ask everyone else to listen. That is what "Shema" means. We say that we believe in one God when we say the Shema, I want us to gesture with our arms as if we are explaining something important to everyone. Ready to say the Shema together? Here we go: "Shema Yisrael, Adonai Elohaynu, Adonai Echad."*

---

[8] <u>Abudraham HaShalem,</u> (Jerusalem: Usha Press, 1963), p.80.

THE EXTENDED SHEMA
FOR ALL AGES

A very purposeful and strong way to recite the Shema is to chant one word for the length of a full breath. No introduction is required. Just begin reciting it this way, strong, slow and confident. People will catch on and join you.

CREATIVE TRANSLATIONS OF THE SHEMA

Creative translations can be a great way of helping people work with ideas they may simply be mouthing by rote. What follows are three translations of the Shema. They can be read as part of the liturgy or studied and compared as part of a lesson.

Creative Translations of the Shema

The Pnai Or Siddur Project

So you shall love what is holy
with all your courage, with all your passion, with all your strength.
Let the words which have come down
shine in our words and our actions.
We must teach our children to know and understand them.
We must speak about what is good and holy in our homes, when we are
working and when we are at play, when we lie down and when we get up.
Let the work of your hands speak them,
let your eyes shine and see with their knowledge.
Let them run in your blood and glow from your doors and windows.

Traditional

You shall love the Lord your God
with all your heart, with all your soul and with all your might.
And these words which I command you on this day
shall be upon your heart.
You shall teach them to your children and speak of them
when you walk upon your path
when you lie down and when you rise up.
You shall bind them as a sign upon your hands
and they shall be for frontlets between your eyes.
You shall write them upon the door posts of your house
and upon your gates.

Translator Unknown

We will love the source of life with all our heart
with all our soul and with all our might.
And these words which we are singing today shall be in our hearts.
We will teach them faithfully to our children.
We will meditate on them both day and night,
at home or on the way, when we lie down and when we rise up.
We will live them through the workings of our hands
and they will guide us as markers on the doorways of our homes
and as signs at the gates of our dwellings.
So we may remember that we are one,
that we may be holy unto the One.

Living Out the Message of the Shema
For all ages

The prayer passage that follows the Shema begins with 16 adjectives. These adjectives describe the qualities of God's message and presence. They also can be presented as a challenge to us! If we embody these qualities, we are god-like. We become partners in God's work on earth. This is the challenge of the Shema.

Each adjective describes a way in which the message of the Shema can be expressed in our lives. The following list is an accessible translation of these 16 adjectives. There are two ways you can use them in class, via discussion or via a quick stylized movement exercise.

Discussion Method:

Leader: *The Shema is such an important prayer for us, it is really the key to Jewish living. The prayer we are going to learn about today is the one that follows the Shema in the morning service. The first 16 words of this prayer are 16 ways in which we can show that we understand and live by the message of the Shema. I am sure that each of you has had a time when you were able to show that you live by the message of the Shema: To love God and to love each other; to love ourselves and to show that lovingness through our day. Today each of you is going to inspire us with times when you did a simple act that showed you understand the message of the Shema.*

We are going to break into small groups now. (Two to four is fine; distribute the 16 adjectives)

Look at the list. Was there a time when you told the truth? A time when you felt loveable? Was there a time when someone was relying on you and you came through for them? These events

may seem small to you, but they are the very ways in which we strengthen ourselves and live by God's message! Share with your group now one of those special times when you lived out the message of the Shema.

DANCE MEDITATION METHOD:

Gather everyone in a circle.

> **LEADER:** *The Shema prayer talks about the many small ways we can express our love for God and each other in our lives: When we sit at home, when we are at school, by how we dress. There are so many ways to show our understanding of the Shema!*
>
> *The prayer which comes right after the Shema in the morning service begins with 16 adjectives, 16 words which describe ways we can behave. Today, we are going to act out those 16 words. We are going to show in our bodies what it means to live by the words of the Shema. There is no "right" position or "wrong." Each of us is just going to show what we think of when we hear these words. Does everyone have enough room? Good. Here are 16 ways we act when we remember the message of the Shema:*

Call out each adjective and instruct the participants to strike a pose or make a motion that represents his or her understanding of the word.

> *To close this activity, you may want to debrief. Ask a few students to talk about the positions that were easy to demonstrate, hard, enjoyable, etc. You may want the group to "try on" each other's positions. You may want to explore why so many people reached upwards when acting out the word "awesome," etc.*

Emet V'yatziv
Sixteen Qualities of God's Teachings
אֱמֶת וְיַצִּיב

Truthful	אֱמֶת
Stable	וְיַצִּיב
Accurate	וְנָכוֹן
Longlasting	וְקַיָּם
Straight	וְיָשָׁר
Trustworthy	וְנֶאֱמָן
Lovable	וְאָהוּב
Affectionate	וְחָבִיב
Delightful	וְנֶחְמָד
Lovely	וְנָעִים
Awesome	וְנוֹרָא
Powerful	וְאַדִּיר
Flexible	וּמְתֻקָּן
Open	וּמְקֻבָּל
Good	וְטוֹב
Beautiful	וְיָפֶה

Gaal Yisrael - A Guided Discussion
For middle school through adult groups

The prayer גָאַל יִשְׂרָאֵל Gaal Yisrael/Redeemer of Israel is recited in every single service between the Shema and the Amidah. What an important place! What can this key prayer be about? There are many reasons we might want to remember the experience of slavery and freedom every day. But perhaps these ideas have a very personal importance, too.

Explain in your own words:

Let's look at the letter Gimel. It means "fair payback." We say that God is Gomel chasadim tovim/He repays kindness with kindness. So gimel means something that happens to us because of our actions.

What is Lamed? It's a tall letter. It means "towards" or "to." The word Lamed means learning or teaching.

Just these two letters together form a different word: Gal, means wave or circle. Gal has the sense of cycle or repeating pattern.

If we read the word Gal at the level of its letters, it means "a pattern that teaches something." How do we experience that? Each of you, in your own thoughts, not out loud, complete the following sentence (somewhat annoyed tone of voice) *"Why do I always...?" "Why does it always seem as though I...?"*

I'm sure every one was able to think of some ending for that sentence. I thought of (... fill in some relevant idea you were working with). (Have people share a few results.)

So these "gal" places, these repeating patterns, these are our personal Egypts, these are the places where we are stuck. The Hebrew word for Egypt is Mitzrayim which means "cramped places!" According to this prayer, how do we move from being stuck to being free? From "gal" to "gaal"? We simple add the Aleph: "A-a-a-h-h-h! I get it! I see God's hand in this. I see the message from the Holy One in this situation." Once that happens, when we start to see the lesson, we really are not so stuck. We are starting to be free from our Egypt.

In small groups now, we are going to talk about a time which is behind us now, some time when we really felt stuck. How did you move past it? What helped you? Time? A special friend? A dream? A new insight?

Share with your group now about a time when you moved from gal/pattern to gaal/freedom.

> *A discussion like this one can help create a strong feeling of connection within a group. You might want to experiment with breaking the group into smaller units, 2 or 3. You may want to keep the whole community together for the debriefing.*

Personalized Hashkiveynu Blessing Activity
For Older Elementary Students Through Adults

The Hashkiveynu prayer follows the evening Shema, coming just before the Amidah. It is a sweet prayer in which we simply ask for safety at night. If you are working in a camp setting, or any time you are with a group near bedtime, Hashkiveynu is a lovely prayer to use as a basis for a personalized blessing.

> **Leader:** *This evening we are going to do something special! We are going to bless each other. I am going to give each of you a copy of part of the evening Shema, the Hashkiveynu paragraph. In this prayer, we simply are asking for a safe and sweet night. Nighttime is a very good time to think good thoughts, isn't it?*
>
> *We aren't just going to read the prayer to each other. We are going to look at the traditional version, but we are going make the blessing more personal. Look at each phrase. How would you say this to your friend in your own words? Is there anything you want to add? Go ahead now, and bless your partner with a safe night.*

LIE US DOWN IN PEACE
הַשְׁכִּיבֵנוּ

Let us lie down in peace our living God
And let us rise up our Source, into life.
Spread over us the tent of your sheltering Presence
And help us find good advice.
Help us so we can help Your good name.
Watch out for us
And guard us from enemies
From confusion
From harm
From hunger
From grief.
Keep obstacles out of our way
Before us and behind us.
Hide us in the wing of Your sheltering care
For You are the One in whom we are safe.
You are kindness and mercy.
Protect us as we come and go
Into life and into peace
From this moment on.
Blessed are You the one
Who guards and guides.

הַשְׁכִּיבֵנוּ ה' אֱלֹהֵינוּ לְשָׁלוֹם, וְהַעֲמִידֵנוּ מַלְכֵּנוּ לְחַיִּים,
וּפְרוֹשׂ עָלֵינוּ סֻכַּת שְׁלוֹמֶךָ, וְתַקְּנֵנוּ בְּעֵצָה טוֹבָה מִלְּפָנֶיךָ,
וְהוֹשִׁיעֵנוּ לְמַעַן שְׁמֶךָ. וְהָגֵן בַּעֲדֵנוּ,
וְהָסֵר מֵעָלֵינוּ אוֹיֵב דֶּבֶר וְחֶרֶב וְרָעָב וְיָגוֹן,
וְהָסֵר שָׂטָן מִלְּפָנֵינוּ וּמֵאַחֲרֵינוּ. וּבְצֵל כְּנָפֶיךָ תַּסְתִּירֵנוּ,
כִּי אֵל שׁוֹמְרֵנוּ וּמַצִּילֵנוּ אָתָּה, כִּי אֵל מֶלֶךְ חַנּוּן וְרַחוּם אָתָּה.
וּשְׁמוֹר צֵאתֵנוּ וּבוֹאֵנוּ לְחַיִּים וּלְשָׁלוֹם מֵעַתָּה וְעַד עוֹלָם:
בָּרוּךְ אַתָּה ה' שׁוֹמֵר עַמּוֹ יִשְׂרָאֵל לָעַד.

The Amidah

Amidah Creative Writing Project
For elementary through adult

Take 19 sheets of paper. At the bottom of each sheet, write one of the chatimot/closing blessings of the Amidah. Distribute the sheets to your group. Instruct people to find a quiet place and to consider the chatimah on their page. Ask them to compose a blessing that thanks God for the blessing mentioned in that chatimah. Use your creative Amidah, the personal prayers followed by the traditional chatimah, for a service or as the basis for a group discussion on themes of the Amidah.

Samples:

"Magen Avraham/Sheild of Abraham:" Thank you God for telling my ancestors to leave Russia so life could be good for me here. We are grateful to you Adonai, our God and Ruler of all, who protected our ancestors Abraham and Sarah.

"Ha-marbeh Lisloach/Forgiveness:" Thank You God for forgiving me even though I am not perfect. You forgive us and let us forgive other people. We praise You God because of Your kindness and forgiveness.

"Shomaya Tefilah/Who hears prayers:" God, our King, Listen to our prayers. Love us and treat us well. We praise You God for hearing the words of our hearts.

AFFIRMATIONS FROM THE SHACHARIT SERVICE
FOR MIDDLE SCHOOL THROUGH ADULTS

The following loosely conveyed themes of the Amidah can be used in several ways. You may use tham as the core paragraph of the brachah followed by the chatimah as part of an educational service. Or you can use the affirmations at a separate time to discuss the themes of the Amidah.

For the discussion method, distribute these creative renditions of the Amidah. Discuss with the group which blessings they really can say with conviction. Are there any blessings that people find less meaningful at this time? Why might you say them anyway?

Affirmations from the Daily Amidah

1. I affirm that I am a spiritual descendent of Abraham, Isaac & Jacob; Sarah, Rivka, Rachel & Leah.
2. I affirm that I am in God's hands in this life and ever after.
3. I affirm that God is All and Holy.
4. I affirm that all humans can acquire wisdom.
5. I affirm that all humans can grow and evolve towards holiness and unity.
6. I affirm that all humans can forgive and heal.
7. I affirm that all who seek God are protected and guided.
8. I affirm that a life in accordance with God's law is a life of health and spirit.
9. I affirm that the hand of the Holy One is visible in the seasons and cycles of nature.
10. I affirm that the Holy One responds to all who reach out.
11. I affirm that the way of the Holy One is justice and right.
12. I affirm that the consequence of evil is evil.
13. I affirm that the Holy One is a support and stronghold for the righteous.
14. I affirm that it is possible to build a House for God, a city of Peace in this world.
15. I affirm that human evolution will yield an era of peace, plenty and safety for all.
16. I affirm that my prayers create ripples of blessings within me and around me.
17. I affirm that God's presence is accessible to us.
18. I affirm that it is pleasant and correct for us to express praise and thanks.
19. I affirm that our struggles to know God's way reveal true peace and joy.

Chatimot from the Daily Amidah

בָּרוּךְ אַתָּה ה׳ מָגֵן אַבְרָהָם.
בָּרוּךְ אַתָּה ה׳ מְחַיֵּה הַמֵּתִים.
בָּרוּךְ אַתָּה ה׳ הָאֵל הַקָּדוֹשׁ.

בָּרוּךְ אַתָּה ה׳ הָאֵל הַקָּדוֹשׁ.
בָּרוּךְ אַתָּה ה׳ הָרוֹצֶה בִּתְשׁוּבָה.
בָּרוּךְ אַתָּה ה׳ חַנּוּן הַמַּרְבֶּה לִסְלֹחַ.
בָּרוּךְ אַתָּה ה׳ גּוֹאֵל יִשְׂרָאֵל.
בָּרוּךְ אַתָּה ה׳ רוֹפֵא חוֹלֵי עַמּוֹ יִשְׂרָאֵל.
בָּרוּךְ אַתָּה ה׳ מְבָרֵךְ הַשָּׁנִים.
בָּרוּךְ אַתָּה ה׳ מְקַבֵּץ נִדְחֵי עַמּוֹ יִשְׂרָאֵל.
בָּרוּךְ אַתָּה ה׳ מֶלֶךְ אוֹהֵב צְדָקָה וּמִשְׁפָּט.
בָּרוּךְ אַתָּה ה׳ שׁוֹבֵר אוֹיְבִים וּמַכְנִיעַ זֵדִים.
בָּרוּךְ אַתָּה ה׳ מִשְׁעָן וּמִבְטָח לַצַּדִּיקִים.
בָּרוּךְ אַתָּה ה׳ בּוֹנֵה יְרוּשָׁלָיִם.
בָּרוּךְ אַתָּה ה׳ מַצְמִיחַ קֶרֶן יְשׁוּעָה.
בָּרוּךְ אַתָּה ה׳ הַמַּחֲזִיר שְׁכִינָתוֹ לְצִיּוֹן.
בָּרוּךְ אַתָּה ה׳ הַטּוֹב שִׁמְךָ וּלְךָ נָאֶה לְהוֹדוֹת.
בָּרוּךְ אַתָּה ה׳ הַמְבָרֵךְ אֶת עַמּוֹ יִשְׂרָאֵל בַּשָּׁלוֹם.

Stepping Into the Presence of God: Movement before the Amidah

For all ages

When we think of prayer, we usually think of saying or singing words. We don't usually think of body movements. However, body movements are involved in Jewish prayer at several different places. One of those places is at the very beginning of each Amidah. Here, we take some steps and we bow. In this exercise, we will concentrate on the steps.

> *Leader, in a calm voice:*
> **Let us all get up and stand in a comfortable way. We need to make sure that there is enough space in front of us and in back of us so that we can each take several steps forward and backward.**

Use one of the relaxation techniques from pages 28-33.

> *In a moment we are going to take three steps backwards from where we are, and then three steps forward to end up exactly where we started. The steps we take help open us up to the presence of God. I will recite each of the words traditionally said as we take each step, one at a time, in Hebrew and in English.*

אֲדֹנָי שְׂפָתַי תִּפְתָּח וּפִי יַגִּיד תְּהִלָּתֶךָ:

Now, let's close our eyes.

Slowly, very slowly, let's move our right leg backwards so that the sole, the tip, of our right foot touches the floor behind us. Slowly, let's roll that foot down and allow the heel of that foot to touch the floor and flatten out, so that we can shift our weight onto that right foot and leg.

Stepping Into the Presence of God: Movement before the Amidah

אֲדֹנָי Adonai-God

And now, slowly, let's move our left leg backwards so that the tip of our left foot touches the floor behind us. Slowly, let's roll that foot down and allow the heel of that foot to touch the floor and flatten out, so that we can shift our weight onto our left foot and leg.

שְׂפָתַי Sefatai-My lips

Finally, continuing slowly, let's move our right leg backwards again so that the tip of our right foot touches the floor behind us. Slowly, let's roll that foot down and allow the heel of that foot to touch the floor and flatten out, so that we can shift our weight onto that right foot and leg.

תִּפְתָּח Tiftach-Open

As we stand here for a few seconds with our eyes closed, and our right leg behind us and our left leg in front of us, let's realize that we are about to walk back to where God was all the time: At the place we started from. Yes, God is right here too, but we are walking to wake us up to where God was all the time.

So. Let's now slowly take our right leg which is behind us and move it forward, setting the heel of our foot in front of us. As we -- ever so slowly now -- roll that foot forward, flattening it out, let's be conscious, let's feel, the muscles in our right leg tightening, working, to bring us closer to God. Good.

וּפִי U'fi-And my mouth

Now let's take our left foot and slowly move it forward, setting the heel of our foot in front of us, and as we flatten it out, let's try to feel the muscles in that leg tightening and working to bring us closer to God.

Stepping Into the Presence of God: Movement before the Amidah

יַגִּיד Yagid—Will tell

Finally, let's take our right foot again, and, in the slowest motion, move it forward, setting the heel of our foot in front of us, right next to our left foot, very close, so that our feet touch. And as we -- ever so slowly now -- roll that foot forward, flattening it out, let's feel the muscles and bones, large and small, and skin, and all the parts of our leg help us move, starting in our heel, moving to our whole foot, to our lower leg, to our thigh and hip, all working to bring us closer to God.

תְּהִלָּתֶךָ Tehilatecha—Your praise

Now we know that our body has brought us back to where God is and always was. With us. And we're ready to daven.

Avot and Imahot Visualization – The Ancestors
For all ages

As we recite "Elohai Avraham, Elohai Yiztchak V'elohai Yaakov..." we will induce a deep personal and intimate connection to the Patriarchs and Matriarchs, our spiritual parents. Each of the ancestors forged a special relationship with God, the same God we turn to now!

Use one of the relaxation techniques from pages 28-33.

> **LEADER: As we stand ready to chant the Amidah, and we think of before Whom we stand, we very naturally think of ourselves as an individual before God. But we are connected to God in a much older and more intimate way than this.**
>
> **As we begin the Amidah, I want to travel back in time together. We are going back to the time of Abraham and Sarah, Issac and Rebeccah, Rachel Leah and Jacob. There are no cars here, no planes, no skyscrapers. People live in simple homes or tents. The clothing is loose and modest.**
>
> **Let's close our eyes. Imagine Abraham and Sarah, starting to daven. It is morning. First light just appeared over the eastern hills. Now the very top of the ball of the sun has risen over the horizon. They stand there, eyes closed, faces turned slightly upward. This is not just a man and a woman from a history book. These are members of our family speaking to their God.**

Pause for ten seconds or so.

> **Let's move forward a bit to the next generation, to Isaac and**

Avot and Imahot Visualization – The Ancestors

Rebecca. We are still in the open plains of Israel, but now the sun is high overhead, just starting to dip to the west. Isaac and Rebecca stand in a field of grain within the shade of several tall leafy trees. Their eyes are closed as they silently thank God. And they plead with God, for their needs and the needs of those they love. Let's stay for a moment with Isaac and Rebecca in prayer.

Pause for about ten seconds.

Let's travel forward one more generation, to the time of Jacob, Rachel and Leah. The sun has set in the land of Israel. It is dark and the stars are scattered across the sky. All three stand near an altar set up by Jacob. Barely aware of each other, they each sway silently and pour out their hearts under the expanse of the sky. They bless and praise and ask for all they need to care for their large family.

Pause for another ten seconds.

Abraham and Isaac and Jacob, Sarah, Rebecca, Rachel and Leah were all praying that we, their children, would continue to face God in praise and prayer. We begin the Amidah, together…

> Such a long introduction is obviously a hefsek/technical break in the flow of prayer outside of an educational setting. If you are using this prayer in a classroom or meditative setting, you may want to adjust the ending slightly and finish by singing Mah Tovu or any other song that evokes images of the ancient Israelites.

Bowing at the Beginning and at the End of the First Bracha: Purposeful Movement/ Guided Meditation
For all ages

In this exercise, we isolate the powerful ritual of bowing before God (הִשְׁתַּחֲוָיָה/hishtachavaya). We concentrate on the meaning of the bowing itself and the three words that accompany it ("Baruch atah Adonai") at the beginning and at the end of the first bracha of the Amidah.

Use one of the relaxation techniques to relax and focus participants from pages 28-33.

Read slowly and in a gentle, calm voice:

> *Instead of beginning the Amidah at the normal pace we are used to, this time, we will slow it down, and concentrate on the bowing at the opening of the Amidah. As we stand, ready to begin the prayer, look around and notice what is all around.* (Here, the group leader can add to or delete from the list of objects that will be listed, as appropriate:) *The walls of this room which are painted white, the pictures on the walls, the ceiling which is also painted white, the lights on the ceiling, the chairs, the people around us and the clothes that they are wearing – the clothes in different colors, and as we look closer to ourselves, we see ourselves, our bodies. We can see our hands and arms, our midsections, our legs and our feet. We see the clothes we are wearing.*

Pause.

> *Each of the things we are looking at may bring to mind thoughts*

Bowing at the Beginning and at the End of the First Bracha: Purposeful Movement/Guided Meditation

related to them. Thoughts related to the other people here perhaps, thoughts related to the clothes we are wearing, maybe even embarrassment at participating in a kind of spiritual exercise we are not used to being part of.

Pause.

I am about to read the traditional six words which we recite before beginning the Amidah. The words which accompany our taking three steps backwards and then three steps forward, so that we end up in the exact spot that we started at. As I read each of the first three words, and I will read them very slowly, let us take a step backwards. At each word, one step backwards:

אֲדֹנָי   *Adonai Oh God*
שְׂפָתַי   *sefatai my lips*
תִּפְתָּח   *tiftach open*

Now, let us all close our eyes. All of the things we were just looking at have disappeared. If I were to ask you to describe which objects we see surrounding us now, we would all probably say "absolutely nothing" because we cannot see anything. Of course, we are not alone. God is with us even though we cannot see God. God is always with us. We just rarely take notice. We are distracted by the things around us. The walls, and the ceiling, and the people, and all the things that surround us. So now we have closed our eyes, and the things around us have disappeared from view. Now, we can concentrate on the one Presence that is always with us but which can never be seen: God's Presence. Even though God is always with us, as I read the next three words of the introduction to the Amidah, let us very slowly take three steps forward as if only now we are truly coming into God's Presence. At each word, take one step forward. And let us continue to keep our eyes closed throughout this exercise.

Bowing at the Beginning and at the End of the First Bracha: Purposeful Movement/Guided Meditation

וּפִי   *U'fi* *And my mouth*

יַגִּיד   *yagid* *will say*

תְּהִלָּתֶךָ   *tehilatecha* *Your praises*

Now we are back where we started, but there is a difference: Now, we are aware that God is with us, God is right in front of us. We are standing directly in front of God right now.

I will not tell us how to envision God, how to think of what God looks like. I will simply ask each of us to know and to feel very strongly that God is right in front of us. It is a very pleasant feeling to be so close to God. God's presence is completely welcoming and warm and embracing and accepting. At the same time, God's presence is majestic and awe-inspiring and totally powerful and infinite and timeless. Try to stay standing for a moment or two focused on God's presence so closely with us. We aren't saying anything to God, but simply trying to feel whatever we feel as we sense God's closeness to us.

Pause.

In a softer voice now:

Now, let us stand with our feet close together and touching each other. Now it is time to respond to God's presence. We will do that by bowing before God. When we bow, we are giving honor and respect to God. We are not merely saying respectful things to God, but we move in a respectful way as well. There are three movements we will do as we bow, and three words which accompany the movements. I'll describe them first:

First, we will bend our knees and say "בָּרוּךְ" (Baruch). "Blessed."

Second, we will bend our upper bodies and heads and say "אַתָּה" (Atah). "are You."

Bowing at the Beginning and at the End of the First Bracha: Purposeful Movement/Guided Meditation

Third, we will stand upright again, and say God's name, "אֲדֹנָי" (Adonai).

As we prepare to bow, let us remember that these three words have been recited by Jews to God since the time of the Bible and for hundreds and hundreds of generations since. So, as we bow and praise God in words not our own, we join with so many Jewish children and parents and grandparents for thousands of years, all over the world who recite these very same words when we realize we have come into the presence of God.

So together now, let us bend our knees, and say... together... "Baruch." And now, together, let us bow our upper bodies and our heads and say "Atah." And finally, let us stand upright and call upon God's name, "Adonai."

Mechalkel Chayim Bechesed: Word Repetition/ Guided Meditation
For Middle School Through Adult

This is an exercise of word-repetition, one of the traditional Jewish ways of meditation. It can be used on its own, that is, not attached to a prayer service, as a means to help us feel the reality that we are, through the life-force in us, connected to God. It is also a very appropriate meditation to be recited as we sit in the synagogue during a repetition of the Amidah. There is a very beautiful and rich phrase often overlooked in the context of a bracha that speaks of the afterlife. Yet its words, "mechalkel chaim bechesed," praise God for the gift of life.

Distribute to each participant a photocopy of the second blessing of the Amidah, (attached, page 114) with the three words of the exercise highlighted in larger type.

Begin with a relaxation exercise, from page pages 28-33. The leader should then tell the group:

> *In a moment, I am going to ask you to read these three words,* מְכַלְכֵּל חַיִּים בְּחֶסֶד *"mechalkel chayim bechesed," slowly, over and over to yourself. You can say them silently or just loud enough for your own ears to hear them, but not loud enough for your neighbor to hear them clearly. As you say these words, I will be reading several different translations of them, slowly, over and over. All of these translations are designed to help us absorb deeply that our lives and our bodies are gifts from God. As you say "mechalkel chaim bechesed" over and over, see if you can eventually have your eyes take leave of the page, and, with your eyes closed, continue to slowly say these words.*
>
> *Please begin to read "mechalkel chaim bechesed" now.*

Mechalkel Chayim Bechesed: Word Repetition/Guided Meditation

Leader continues:

God gives us our life with love. God sustains our life-force with grace. God grants us our energy in lovingkindness. God supplies our health with a parent's love. God offers wholeness to us as a gift. God heals our bodies with a whole heart. God gives us God's own breath out of love. God transfers to us God's own spark of life in kindness. God enriches our lives with love. God gives us completeness as a blessing. God bestows upon us healing in lovingkindness.

This paragraph should be repeated up to 6 times. You can add or simplify the language for a younger group. At some point in the repetition, the leader may choose to remind people of the kavanah.

"As you continue to repeat "mechalkel chayim bechesed," feel how your every breath comes from God, know that the pulse within your heart and throughout your body is supplied by God".

Gently end the exercise or move to the next portion of the service by reciting the chatimah.

מְכַלְכֵּל חַיִּים בְּחֶסֶד

WHO SUSTAINS LIFE WITH LOVINGKINDNESS

אַתָּה גִבּוֹר לְעוֹלָם אֲדֹנָי, מְחַיֵּה מֵתִים אַתָּה רַב לְהוֹשִׁיעַ.
מְכַלְכֵּל חַיִּים בְּחֶסֶד, מְחַיֵּה מֵתִים בְּרַחֲמִים רַבִּים, סוֹמֵךְ נוֹפְלִים
וְרוֹפֵא חוֹלִים וּמַתִּיר אֲסוּרִים,
וּמְקַיֵּם אֱמוּנָתוֹ לִישֵׁנֵי עָפָר.
מִי כָמוֹךָ בַּעַל גְּבוּרוֹת וּמִי דוֹמֶה לָּךְ,
מֶלֶךְ מֵמִית וּמְחַיֶּה וּמַצְמִיחַ יְשׁוּעָה.
וְנֶאֱמָן אַתָּה לְהַחֲיוֹת מֵתִים.
בָּרוּךְ אַתָּה ה' מְחַיֵּה הַמֵּתִים.

THE KEDUSHAH I: WORD REPETITION/GUIDED MEDITATION

FOR ALL AGES

The Kedushah was composed originally by ancient Jewish mystics. They constructed a prayer around two of the most highly treasured images of God that the Bible records: The prophets Isaiah and Ezekiel[9] each are granted what appears to be a direct vision of God! One goal of these ancient rabbinic mystics was to induce a similar vision themselves. What better way to achieve that then to use the words left behind by two of the most gifted and divinely favored Prophets of Israel? And yet, when the Kedushah is recited in our day, the experience most of us have is empty of mysticism.

This exercise is based on some of the original versions of the Kedushah, which include manifold repetitions of the famous words that the Prophets heard angels chant (especially "Kadosh, kadosh, kadosh," "Holy, holy, holy"). Its aim is to restore a mystical experience to our recitation of the Kedushah.

Use one of the relaxation exercises to relax and focus the participants.

> *LEADER: Let us all close our eyes. We will take a journey now. This is not a journey outward and away, but inward. The mystics teach that our souls are connected directly to God. In fact the Zohar teaches that our souls are constructed out of the throne of God. Our souls are connected in a direct way to the throne of God. That means that the throne of God is as close to us as our own souls. So we need to take an inward journey to where our soul resides and to find that hidden pathway that leads to the throne of God. It is not far; we carry it with us always.* (Pause). *And so, again, we will take a journey towards God's throne not*

---

[9] Isaiah 6:3, and Ezekiel chapters 1-3

outward and away, but inward. We will follow the path recorded by the prophet Isaiah and followed by countless Jewish mystics.

Let's take a deep breath in and let it out.

Let us imagine ourselves entering a space in the back of our consciousness (for children: in the back of our minds). At first it is dark and empty. But then we perceive something: It is filled with sound. Chanting, singing... of angels!

The angels surround the center of the space -- all around it, and above and below it. And in the center is the throne with God upon it. Try as we might, we can only see the back of the throne. But we know and we feel God's presence upon it. And we hear the words of the angels as Isaiah heard them too (very slowly):

קָדוֹשׁ, קָדוֹשׁ, קָדוֹשׁ, ה' צְבָאוֹת, מְלֹא כָל הָאָרֶץ כְּבוֹדוֹ

"Kadosh, Kadosh, Kadosh, Adonai Tzeva'ot,
Melo Chol Ha-aretz Kevodo."

"Holy, holy, holy, God of constellations,
the whole world is full of God's glory."

We are privileged to see and to hear. Because it is not so far away. The throne is attached to our own soul. And so, we are welcome here. The angels are filled with happiness. They are filled with contentment. All of their needs are met because they are in the presence of God. And so they delight in God and chant these words of praise and joy. We too feel so satisfied. There is nothing that we need when we are so close to God, to the source of our souls. We too join in chanting the words of the angels.

The Kedushah I: Word Repetition/Guided Meditation

In a moment, we will chant -- so slowly -- these words. If you know all the words by heart, then join me in saying them. If not, then simply repeat "Kadosh, Kadosh, Kadosh," and don't worry about reciting the last few words. Let us keep our attention in that space in the back of our minds, in God's presence as we recite, seven times, slowly, the words that express our soulful, gentle, fully satisfied contentedness. We chant just loudly enough for us to hear ourselves, but not loudly enough for those around us to hear:

1 - קָדוֹשׁ, קָדוֹשׁ, קָדוֹשׁ, ה' צְבָאוֹת, מְלֹא כָל הָאָרֶץ כְּבוֹדוֹ.
"Kadosh, Kadosh, Kadosh,
Adonai Tzeva'ot, Melo Chol Ha-aretz Kevodo."

2 - קָדוֹשׁ, קָדוֹשׁ, קָדוֹשׁ, ה' צְבָאוֹת, מְלֹא כָל הָאָרֶץ כְּבוֹדוֹ.
"Kadosh, Kadosh, Kadosh,
Adonai Tzeva'ot, Melo Chol Ha-aretz Kevodo."

3 - קָדוֹשׁ, קָדוֹשׁ, קָדוֹשׁ, ה' צְבָאוֹת, מְלֹא כָל הָאָרֶץ כְּבוֹדוֹ.
"Kadosh, Kadosh, Kadosh,
Adonai Tzeva'ot, Melo Chol Ha-aretz Kevodo."

4 - קָדוֹשׁ, קָדוֹשׁ, קָדוֹשׁ, ה' צְבָאוֹת, מְלֹא כָל הָאָרֶץ כְּבוֹדוֹ.
"Kadosh, Kadosh, Kadosh,
Adonai Tzeva'ot, Melo Chol Ha-aretz Kevodo."

5 - קָדוֹשׁ, קָדוֹשׁ, קָדוֹשׁ, ה' צְבָאוֹת, מְלֹא כָל הָאָרֶץ כְּבוֹדוֹ.
"Kadosh, Kadosh, Kadosh,
Adonai Tzeva'ot, Melo Chol Ha-aretz Kevodo."

6 - קָדוֹשׁ, קָדוֹשׁ, קָדוֹשׁ, ה' צְבָאוֹת, מְלֹא כָל הָאָרֶץ כְּבוֹדוֹ.
"Kadosh, Kadosh, Kadosh,
Adonai Tzeva'ot, Melo Chol Ha-aretz Kevodo."

7 - קָדוֹשׁ, קָדוֹשׁ, קָדוֹשׁ, ה' צְבָאוֹת, מְלֹא כָל הָאָרֶץ כְּבוֹדוֹ.
"Kadosh, Kadosh, Kadosh,
Adonai Tzeva'ot, Melo Chol Ha-aretz Kevodo."

We linger just a few seconds longer in this space in silence, observing the angels and the throne before we take our leave.
(Pause for a few seconds).

Now, we journey back to the front of our consciousness (for children: to the front of our minds)***, where the chanting of the angels is only a distant echo. And slowly, we open our eyes.***

THE KEDUSHAH II: WORD REPETITION/ GUIDED MEDITATION
FOR ALL AGES

Use one of the relaxation techniques from pages 28-33 to begin the exercise.

> *LEADER: Let us close our eyes. Let us imagine[10] that we begin to see the heavens in the distance above us. There is a storm approaching, but it is far away. We can see the swirling clouds and darkened sky, and it is coming closer. Somehow, though, we are attracted to it; it does not feel dangerous. Lightning is visible now too. Every so often, the whole sky lights up, lines of whiteness pierce the sky. We continue to look, and it continues to approach. The colors of fire are visible in the sky: orange, red, and yellow. And subtler hues as well: pastel pinks, soft yellows, and electrum. There is movement in the center of this unusual system, and it invites our eye.*
>
> *Now, we see what the movement is. There appears to be a small herd of animals there. Included among the animals are humans too. And it feels like a dream: Although the vision might make no sense in real life, here, in this celestial cloud-swirl, it all seems to fit. Just as things we see in a dream somehow make sense, even though they wouldn't really make sense in our waking hours.*

---

[10] The vision of Ezekiel is found in the Book of Ezekiel, chapters 1-3. The verse we are focusing on is Ezekiel 3:12. The vision of Moses is found in the Book of Exodus, 24:9-18. This translation of Ezekiel 3:12 is based on the new Jewish Publication Society translation, <u>Tanakh: The Holy Scriptures</u>, 1985, "Blessed is the Presence of the LORD, in His Place." I have substituted "God's" for "His." Two interesting alternate translations which are inspirational, if less literal: <u>The Weekday Prayer Book</u>, edited by Gershon Hadas in 1974, p.55, translates "Praised be the glory of God from on high!" <u>Siddur Sim Shalom</u>, edited by Jules Harlowe in 1985, p. 109, renders: "Praised be the glory of the Lord throughout the universe."

Creatures of the earth: some from the wild, and some that live among people; some that walk on all fours, and some with feathered wings. People among them as well. They all come into better focus now. We can see that they are all moving as one.

As it all comes closer, we see that this small herd is, in fact, just four angels with wings, attached one to the other. And each one has the faces of four: The face of a human being, the face of a lion, the face of an ox, and the face of an eagle. The world's creatures -- wild and domestic -- seem to be living in heaven as they live on earth. Only in heaven, in this vision, they are all united in their closeness to God.

And above them are the clouds of heaven. We keep getting closer. The clouds appear, closer up, almost as a great glacier of ice. Just below them, the angels, creatures of God all of them, united together, seem to be holding up the icy blue-white frost and haze with their backs, with their hands, with their wings. And above the blue-white mist is the throne. It too is bluish-white, jewel-like, resembling a sapphire. Moses saw this. Ezekiel too. It was God's throne. The flashes of lightning and colors of fire came from here. And from below, we see the back of the throne.

Now we come even closer, and we are conscious of the sound that had begun when we observed the world of the animals moving together. A rushing sound. A sound of great waters. A sound of wings. But now the family of angels has stopped moving, and their sound has stopped too.

And we are lifted up! And our spirits are lifted up. We are no longer just viewing this vision; now we are part of it. And we ascend higher than the creatures, high enough to see the throne. I'll ask us all now to slowly take in a deep breath, and to slowly

The Kedushah II: Word Repetition/Guided Meditation

let it out. Because we feel we have come into the presence of God. We are above the icy blue mist, together with the throne. And we can breathe so easily now because we know we are in the safe presence of God, the Parent of all of us, the Parent of all creatures, who cares for us all so much.

From behind us we hear a sound. It is the sound of words. Words from...somewhere, expressing joy of being with God:

בָּרוּךְ כְּבוֹד ה' מִמְּקוֹמוֹ:
"Baruch Kevod Adonai Mimkomo."
"Blessed is the Presence of God, in God's Place."

In this great realm, lifted up high, in the awesome and wonderful dream-storm, we feel the closeness of our Creator and the closeness of all beings on earth. We will join the voice praising God and we chant slowly, just loudly enough for us to hear ourselves, but not loudly enough for those around us to hear. We will join the voice and say: "Baruch kevod Adonai mimkomo." We will say it, with our eyes still closed-- from this lofty realm -- seven times so very slowly. Let's begin now:

1 - בָּרוּךְ כְּבוֹד ה' מִמְּקוֹמוֹ:
"Baruch Kevod Adonai Mimkomo."
2 - בָּרוּךְ כְּבוֹד ה' מִמְּקוֹמוֹ:
"Baruch Kevod Adonai Mimkomo."
3 - בָּרוּךְ כְּבוֹד ה' מִמְּקוֹמוֹ:
"Baruch Kevod Adonai Mimkomo."
4 - בָּרוּךְ כְּבוֹד ה' מִמְּקוֹמוֹ:
"Baruch Kevod Adonai Mimkomo."
5 - בָּרוּךְ כְּבוֹד ה' מִמְּקוֹמוֹ:
"Baruch Kevod Adonai Mimkomo."
6 - בָּרוּךְ כְּבוֹד ה' מִמְּקוֹמוֹ:
"Baruch Kevod Adonai Mimkomo."

7 - ‎בָּרוּךְ כְּבוֹד ה׳ מִמְּקוֹמוֹ:
"Baruch Kevod Adonai Mimkomo."

Slowly now, we descend from the heights and from the storm. We come back to the ground. And the cloud formation drifts high and away... Slowly, we open our eyes.

Birkat Chonen Ha-da'at: Guided Meditation
For all ages

This bracha expresses our praise to God who has granted us intelligence. But it also does more than that. It asks God for knowledge: "חָנֵּנוּ מֵאִתְּךָ דֵּעָה בִּינָה וְהַשְׂכֵּל/Chonenu mei'itcha de'ah, binah, vehaskeil," "Grant us knowledge, discernment and wisdom." This doesn't necessarily mean, "God, make us smarter." One of the things it can mean is "God, give me the knowledge to solve a problem that I am facing." That is, it isn't only a request for general intelligence, but also a request for very specific help. And that is what this exercise is based upon. We can use this beracha, as we daven the Amidah, as a way to ask God's help in solving conflicts, doubts and problems that we face.

Spend some time with the group to begin to think of an issue they could use God's help in solving. They will be called on to silently and privately present that problem to God. It can be a conflict with parents or children or other relatives or friends. It can be a problem we have with ourselves. It can be doubts we have about what to do in another area of life.

Distribute copies of this bracha (see page 126). Lead one of the relaxation exercises, pages 28-33.

> *LEADER: In this exercise, we are going to ask God to give us the knowledge to solve a problem that we are facing. We should keep in mind that God doesn't usually answer us in words, the way people do. God often plants an answer directly in our hearts. We may sense that answer immediately, as part of our praying to God. Sometimes we may not discover that answer until later. It may take several attempts at asking before we find the path that God is showing us. Also, like other kinds of exercise, this exercise may take practice for it to work well. The key is focusing. Focusing clearly on communicating one problem to God and then being open to an answer. We'll do it together today, but I encourage you to try this often on your own.*

Birkat Chonen Ha-da'at: Guided Meditation

Let's slowly read together the first part of the bracha; we'll pause just before we get to the word "baruch."

אַתָּה חוֹנֵן לְאָדָם דַּעַת וּמְלַמֵּד לֶאֱנוֹשׁ בִּינָה:
"Atah chonen l'adam da'at u'melamed l'enosh bina.

חָנֵּנוּ מֵאִתְּךָ דֵעָה בִּינָה וְהַשְׂכֵּל
Chonenu mei'itcha de'ah, binah, vehaskail."

"You graciously endow mortals with intelligence, teaching wisdom and understanding. Grant us knowledge, discernment and wisdom."

At this point, let's close our eyes. Let us now focus on one problem we want to ask God's help in solving. Let us try and see as clearly as we can what it is that is bothering us, and keep that in our minds for a moment or two. Let us face and feel the discomfort it may cause us and the fullness of the doubts we have as to how to deal with our issue. (Pause for half a minute or so). **Now, without entirely letting go of the difficulty we have presented to God, let us open ourselves. God may point us in a direction. God may give us a hint, now or later. Let us stay open, eyes closed, contented that God has heard us. We cannot force God to answer us; but if we have called upon God in truth, then God is close; help is close to us. We will stay in this close embrace with God for another moment or two.** (Pause for half a minute or so).

Now, let us open our eyes and gently stretch. Let's conclude by thanking God for hearing us. Let's read the ending of the bracha together:

בָּרוּךְ אַתָּה ה' חוֹנֵן הַדָּעַת:
"Baruch atah Adonai, Chonen Ha-da'at."

"Praised are You, God who graciously grants knowledge."
Let's open our eyes. Did we feel God's closeness? Do we feel pointed in a direction? Let's remain open for guidance from God on what we have presented. And let's keep in mind that "calling upon God in truth" (Psalm 145:18, in the "Ashrei"), may take some practice.

חוֹנֵן הַדָּעַת
Birkat Chonen Ha-da'at

אַתָּה חוֹנֵן לְאָדָם דַּעַת וּמְלַמֵּד לֶאֱנוֹשׁ בִּינָה:
חָנֵּנוּ מֵאִתְּךָ דֵּעָה בִּינָה וְהַשְׂכֵּל

*"Atah chonen l'adam da'at u'melamed l'enosh bina
Chonenu mei'itcha de'ah, binah, vehaskail."*

"You graciously endow mortals with intelligence, teaching wisdom and understanding. Grant us knowledge, discernment and wisdom."

בָּרוּךְ אַתָּה ה'. חוֹנֵן הַדָּעַת:

"Baruch atah Adonai, Chonen Ha-da'at."

"Praised are You, God who graciously grants knowledge."

Birkat Ha-rotzeh B'tshuvah: A Writing Exercise on Teshuvah on Yom Kippur Katan

For all ages

In this bracha we ask God to help us do "teshuvah," to help us "return" to our better selves and to God. The bracha ends with the words "Baruch Atah Ha-shem, Ha-rotzeh B'tshuvah," "Blessed are You, God, Who wants (or welcomes) Teshuvah."

Often, when we say this bracha during the Amidah quickly, it is difficult to focus on how we may need to return to our better selves and to God. And yet, the bracha declares that God "wants" our teshuvah. God has provided us with many opportunities for teshuva: One familiar time for teshuvah is during the High Holidays: Rosh Hashanah and Yom Kippur. But those holidays only come once a year. Another opportunity is each time we recite the Amidah and we reach this bracha. But, as we said above, it can be hard to truly consider how we need to do teshuva as we quickly say the words of the Amidah.

There is another opportunity we have to do teshuva that comes more often than the High Holidays. That is on Yom Kippur Katan, or "Little Yom Kippur." According to Jewish tradition, the day before Rosh Chodesh (the first day of each Hebrew month) is called Yom Kippur Katan, and is a time to focus on teshuva. Just as we do teshuva each Yom Kippur in order to start the new year with a new, righteous beginning, so too, we do teshuva each Yom Kippur Katan in order to start each new month with a new, righteous beginning.

Instructions for the Exercise

On Yom Kippur Katan, distribute a small piece of paper and pencils as needed to each student. Ask each student to review the last month. Challenge them to think of one change that they might want to make in the way they were in this last month. It could concern the way they related to their parents, their siblings or other relatives, their teachers, or friends. It could have to do with the way they related to themselves: Did they disappoint themselves in one way by doing too much of one thing or not enough or another? Emphasize

Birkat Ha-rotzeh B'tshuvah: A Writing Exercise on Teshuvah on Yom Kippur Katan

that they are being asked to come up with only one thing that they might want to change from the way they were in the past month.

Ask them to write that one thing down on the slip of paper, and then fold the paper in half and write their names on the cover. Ask the participants to respect each other's privacy, and not to try and read what others have written. Tell them that no one will read what they are writing, not even you, the leader. Explain that you will collect the slips of paper, put them all into a large envelope, and keep the envelope for one month. Tell them that you will give these slips back to them next Yom Kippur Kattan. At that time, they will have a chance to evaluate the extent to which they have indeed done teshuva on the one thing they hoped to change from the previous month. The papers should ideally be distributed just before the students begin to daven. The participants should be reminded that it ought to be easier to pay special attention to Birkat Ha-rotzeh B'tshuva as they daven this day.

HA-ROTZEH B'TSHUVA: A GUIDED MEDITATION ON FORGIVENESS
FOR ALL AGES

This is a guided meditation on forgiveness. It can be done privately or in a group. It can be a useful portion of a healing service. The theme of forgiveness is also part of the early morning service (when we accept the mitzvah of loving everyone), the bedtime Shema, the months of Elul and Tishrei and any Rosh Chodesh, or during the Rotzeh B'tshuvah section of the daily Amidah.

In the preliminary daily prayers of traditional practitioners, there is a line that says "My God the soul which you placed in me, she is pure," or more simply, the soul is pure. In Hebrew the words are, אֱלֹהַי נְשָׁמָה שֶׁנָּתַתָּ בִּי טְהוֹרָה הִיא Elohai neshamah shenatata bi tehora he.

The following meditation practice focuses on this phrase and the idea behind it: No matter what we do in this life, the soul within us remains pure. Moreover, no matter whom we encounter, whatever their outward presentation, whatever their personality or history, within each is a pure soul. Once we fully understand this, our relationship with others and ourselves can be altered, often dramatically.

For each of the following steps, give participants at least a few minutes. Take as much time as you think the group needs.

1. Begin with the basic sitting technique: relaxed, eyes closed, sitting fairly straight without effort, breathing normally, noticing the rising and falling of the chest with the breath.
2. Imagine that you are able to watch yourself in a mirror as others see you, and notice that there are many places of imperfection. Sometimes we act foolishly, sometimes we say silly things, and sometimes we realize that our thoughts are not very kind. Indeed, sometimes our thoughts are quite bizarre.
3. As you observe within, notice that you find some things about yourself that are humorous while other things are somewhat unlikable. Notice your feelings.
4. Now, pretend that there is a magic filter between you and the mirror so

that you cannot see the normal reflection in front of you, but only a soul as you would imagine it. Assume this is like a spiritual x-ray machine. You can still see your shape, you can still hear your voice, but the dominant experience is that you are looking straight into your own soul. Notice that self-judgement and self-criticism are not connected with the soul level.

5. Now, remove the filter and replace your own image with someone else. Try to imagine somebody with whom you have had problems, or with whom you recently argued. Remembering and reviewing some incident from the past, look and listen carefully as you experience your feelings towards this person.

6. Once again, place the filter between yourself and this person and say to yourself, "The soul is pure." Notice any change in your feelings towards this person now that you are observing his or her soul.

7. Allow as many people as you wish to appear before you, and then observe them through the filter that says, "The soul is pure." Do this for a number of people with whom you may have had difficult relations. Continue with as many images as you wish until the time for meditation is over.

This meditation is extraordinarily useful for opening the heart. It quickly reveals a greater truth behind the illusion of life, and it teaches us to look more carefully at people and situations; to transcend, to the extent possible, personality and ego.

After some practice, this is a wonderful meditation to take with you into daily life. For each person that you encounter, whether a friend or a total stranger, allow yourself to silently say "Tehora he," or "This soul is pure." That is all you need to do for this practice. Do it regularly and you will quickly find your heart opening. Whenever we acknowledge other souls, we experience our own; moreover, our hearts cannot help but be open when we are in touch with our souls. Try it and see.

Birkat Rofeh Cholei Amo Yisrael: A Guided Visualization*

FOR ALL AGES
*This guided meditation is included on the accompanying tape

There are two ways that this meditation can be applied: for one's self or for others. For both, the exercise involves repeating over and over the first few words of this bracha from the Amidah as we keep in mind whatever needs healing. This can be a specific part of our bodies or our emotional health, or the whole person in general. The words are:

רְפָאֵנוּ ה׳ וְנֵרָפֵא הוֹשִׁיעֵנוּ וְנִוָּשֵׁעָה

Refa'enu Adonai Venerafeh; Hoshi'enu Veivashe'a
Heal us God and we shall be healed, Save us and we shall be saved.

It was the prophet Jeremiah[11] who first prayed these words to God. He was feeling terribly alone. He felt that no one understood his pain. And so he turned directly to God and asked for healing. This exercise helps to put us in touch with God's healing presence which is always there, but which we usually ignore. As with all of these spiritual exercises, the more one practices, the more one will feel the results.

One of the relaxation exercises from pages 28-33 can be used.

> **LEADER:** *This is an exercise in physical or emotional healing using prayer. We will visualize healing for the body (physical well-being) or soul (emotional well being), for ourselves or for others as we recite the beginning of the Healing blessing from the Amidah.*
>
> *It helps to visualize the healing in as much detail as possible. For example, if you are recovering from a broken elbow, you can*

---

[11] See Jeremiah 17:14. In the book of Jeremiah, the words are in the singular. The sages of the Talmud set the verse in the plural in the Amidah to accord with the general custom of framing prayers in a communal form.

Birkat Rofeh Cholei Amo Yisrael: A Guided Visualization

imagine the pain leaving or "melting" away from your elbow as you say the words of the blessing. If you are praying for someone else's healing, you can picture that person as relieved and healed from the suffering he or she feels as you recite the words.

In a moment, we will recite the blessing over and over as we try to imagine healing. Begin by reading the words on the attached page. After a while, if you are able to say the words by heart, close your eyes as you recite.

Let us begin to say the blessing very slowly and only loud enough for our own ears to hear it as we visualize the healing for which we are praying, in as much detail as we can:

Refa'enu Adonai VeNerafeh   רְפָאֵנוּ ה׳ וְנֵרָפֵא
Hoshi'enu veNivashe'ah.   הוֹשִׁיעֵנוּ וְנִוָּשֵׁעָה
Refa'enu Adonai VeNerafeh   רְפָאֵנוּ ה׳ וְנֵרָפֵא
Hoshi'enu veNivashe'ah.   הוֹשִׁיעֵנוּ וְנִוָּשֵׁעָה
Refa'enu Adonai VeNerafeh   רְפָאֵנוּ ה׳ וְנֵרָפֵא
Hoshi'enu veNivashe'ah.   הוֹשִׁיעֵנוּ וְנִוָּשֵׁעָה
Refa'enu Adonai VeNerafeh   רְפָאֵנוּ ה׳ וְנֵרָפֵא
Hoshi'enu veNivashe'ah.   הוֹשִׁיעֵנוּ וְנִוָּשֵׁעָה
Refa'enu Adonai VeNerafeh   רְפָאֵנוּ ה׳ וְנֵרָפֵא
Hoshi'enu veNivashe'ah.   הוֹשִׁיעֵנוּ וְנִוָּשֵׁעָה

Continue very slowly for two minutes or more.

HEALING MEDITATIONS
MISHEBERACH L'CHOLIM
FOR ALL AGES

When we understand and truly feel the words of our prayers, we are experiencing powerful prayer. We can obviously simply recite our prayers with little feeling or understanding. Conversely, we may have very strong feelings, but lack the means to put them into the context of prayer.

For this reason, the power of prayers for healing can be easily appreciated When our loved ones are ill, we have no lack of strong feeling! In prayers for healing, formulaic or freely created, the words and the emotion flow together to provide comfort and hope.

There is a second aspect of prayers for healing that can help those who are ill and their caretakers. Prayers for healing are public acts. When the community hears that one of their members is healing from heart surgery or coping with a fall, the community is aware that their help is needed. The concern and active support of one's community, during the time of illness or crisis are all part of the rich fabric of a nourishing Jewish life.

The following exercise can be used in a traditional service as well as a special "healing service" format. The standard procedure of calling people up to the bimah, and asking them to recite the name of their loved one is preserved. The exercise may be more appropriate for a smaller community; personalizing the praying in this way adds quite a bit of time to the service.

> **LEADER:** *During the Misheberach, we ask for God's blessings and presence for our loved ones. Each of us in a praying community agrees to function like a satellite dish, reaching for God's blessing and sending it out to our friends who are ill or suffering.*
>
> *We pray for one thing when a person is very close to death. We pray for different things if someone is recovering from a complicated surgery and yet something else when a person is facing a long stretch of dependence or decline. We may wish to*

bless someone with emotional healing, or physical healing or both.

If you are asking for a Misheberach today, please think for a moment about the person for whose healing you are praying. How would you like this community to direct its attention? (It is useful here to give a real example, such as "I'll be asking for your support for Sayde bat Ester. I'd like to ask you to pray with me that she feel love and comfort from those around her as she faces the challenges ahead.") *As you formulate this kavanah, this healing intention, please do not violate the person's privacy. Phrase your blessing in a way that preserves the person's dignity. Try to formulate one sentence that expresses the healing intent you want us to hold today.*

Come on up now. Say the person's name in English or Hebrew. Traditionally, we give the Hebrew name as so-and-so the son or daughter of...and give the mother's name. Whatever name you have for the person is fine though.

Have people stand around and say their name and their sentence. It may be appropriate to offer handholding or hugs to the people who are asking for healing prayers.

If you are praying with a large congregation, a long list can be quite tedious. Perhaps having each person rise and say the name from their place would be more appropriate.

Conclude with a traditional Misheberach formula and/or one of the beautiful healing songs by Debbie Freidman, Rabbi Shefa Gold, Rabbi Aryeh Hirschfield or others. See the Resources Appendix for tapes.

Korbanot Meditation
For teens through adults

Korbanot/ritual offerings are part of the daily liturgy (in Birchot Ha-shachar and the Retzai blessing of the Amidah), the holiday and Shabbat Musaf and on Rosh Chodesh. The whole of tefilah in fact, is based on the sacrificial cycle at the holy Temple. As hard as it may be to relate to the idea of animal sacrifice today, the power of transforming something concrete into a gift to God is still a concept we can appreciate. The following is a meditation on korbanot that can be adjusted for use on various occasions.

Use one of the relaxation techniques on pages 28-33 to relax and focus the participants.

> *LEADER: Today we are going to imagine the act of offering a gift up to God. Scan your body mentally as the breath pours into each limb, nourishing each limb. Breathe deeply.*
>
> *This body is your "animal," your animate, physical self. Each day when the Temple stood, we offered an animal sacrifice to God. Today we are going to offer part of our self. Continue to breathe deeply. We are going to agree today to use our life energy to do God's will. Choose a quality or strength that you have that you can offer up to holy service today. It could be your insight. It could be your physical strength. It could be your singing voice, part of the income from your work, your compassion. We are going to dedicate, raise up that quality or strength. In the ancient temple, these gifts were placed on the mizbeach/altar. The flame on that altar was originally lit by a light that descended from heaven. The flame was lit by God and kept alive by our priests. Imagine that flame that touches both heaven and earth. Hold your offering into that flame. Feel your gift being accepted. You are infused with that light. Your gift is dedicated, raised up. The blessings that God has given you, you are now sharing back*

with all of creation. See yourself today as a holy instrument to do God's will.

May the words of our mouths and the meditations of our hearts be acceptable before You, dear God.

Amen

Alternatives: This meditation is based on the Tamid, the daily morning and afternoon offering. Korbanot/offerings with particular spiritual purposes were offered on Shabbat, the New Moons, and other holidays. There is also a set of offerings that is neither seasonal nor communal. Several moments of personal transformation (such as great joy or remorse or cleansing from certain physical traumas) were also marked by specific offerings. You can adjust the kavanah of the guided meditation to suit the season or the event.

Purposeful Movement:
Modim Anachnu Lach
For all ages

Toward the end of the Amidah[12], there is a blessing whose theme is thanks to God. Its first word, "modim" and its last word "lehodot," both connect with the idea of thanks (they are both related grammatically to "todah," "thank you."). At the very beginning of this blessing, at its first word, "Modim," we bow in thanks. Thanks that God has heard the prayers that we have said up to this point in the Amidah.. We give thanks that God's wonders are with us every day, morning, noon, and night, as the blessing puts it. This exercise challenges us to personalize the gratitude. It asks us to bow slowly with willing heart as we reflect on at least one thing for which are truly grateful to God.

There is a hint of the importance of the bowing in this blessing in a discussion in the Talmud (Bava Kamma 16a, very bottom). There, the Sages are trying to define a certain animal, a "Bardelus." Each Sage identified it so differently, it seemed as if they weren't even talking about the same animal. The definitions ranged from a panther to a hyena to a snake, among others! They wondered whether, in fact, this "Bardelus" transformed itself every few years (they guessed every seven years) into a different form, and perhaps that was why each Sage described it so differently.

In the midst of this discussion, seemingly out of nowhere, the Sages mention that it isn't only the "Bardelus" that changes its form every few years. Human beings too, the Sages claimed, change form. Our backbone can become crooked and bent out of shape, they said, and can resemble the curved shape of a snake... But only when we do not bow our backs as we say the blessing beginning with the word "Modim" in the Amidah!

This is our Sages' way of emphasizing the importance of never letting a day go by, no matter how difficult, without finding something for which to thank God, of not standing up so straight with pride, without bowing in gratefulness to the Source of All.

One of the commentators on the Talmud makes mention of an opinion that the snake in the Garden of Eden originally walked completely upright. Originally, it had legs and was able to walk upright like a human being. Its punishment – the removal of its legs so that it had to move on its belly

---

[12]At the beginning of the second to the last blessing of each and every Amidah.

without the ability to ever stand erect -- was given because the snake was so ungrateful for what it already had. It always wanted more.[13]

> *LEADER: Let's practice bowing at the word Modim with the goal of achieving true gratefulness and humility before God. I'd like to ask everyone to stand. Place yourself so that there is plenty of space between you and the people standing around you. You shouldn't feel crowded or that you might bump into someone else if you should move at all.*

Use one of the relaxation techniques on pages 28-33 to relax and focus the participants.

> *Keep your eyes closed. I will describe what we are going to do in this exercise. First listen; do not yet do what I am about to describe. All we are going to do in this exercise is very slowly bow from the waist as we recite, with great concentration and intention, the words "Modim anachnu lach/We are grateful to You." That's it. But we are going to take our time doing this.*
>
> *There are two steps. First, we need to think of at least one thing for which we are truly grateful to God. Second, is to keep your focus on that thing for which we are grateful to God as we bow from the waist and recite "Modim anachnu lach."*
>
> *At first think of only one thing for which you are grateful. As you practice this exercise over and over, you may well be able to advance to that stage wherein you'll be able to truly thank God for several things at the very same time as you bow to God. Some possibilities for the kinds of the things to thank God for in this blessing are:*
>
> > *•Thanks that God has heard and accepted all the prayers we have offered in the Amidah up to this point.*

---
[13]Maharsha on Bava Kamma 19a who cites Sotah 9b.

- *Thanks for the "small miracles" which accompany us almost routinely every day, "erev vavoker vetzohorayim," "morning, noon, and night," as the words of this blessing put it.*

- *Which aspects of our daily life do we (or perhaps should we) feel grateful for, even though we experience them every day? These may include being close to people we love; experiencing good health; enjoying a warm and pleasant home, and good, plentiful, and nourishing food; appreciating the beauty of nature which surrounds us, including the warmth of the sun and the beauty of whatever features of the earth are near us (the ocean, rivers, mountains, hills, trees, flowers, and so on).*

- *Anything else that each of us may think of that may motivate us to give thanks to God.*

So, let's try it. Let's stand the way we do when we recite the Amidah, with our feet placed closely together. Now, think of one thing for which we really do feel honestly grateful to God. As we hold that inside of us, we are going to bow -- not yet, but in a moment -- before God as we recite -- very slowly -- "Modim anachnu lach."

We are going to bow in three fluid stages, without really stopping the movement between them. We continue to keep our eyes closed to help us concentrate on gratefulness. Now, I am going to ask us to say in a quiet voice the first of the Hebrew words "Modim anachnu lakh;" let us say the word "Modim," and, slowly, bow our backs slightly forward. Without stopping, but continuing so slowly, let's bow forward a little more as we say the word "anachnu," and finally, continuing to bow without stopping. In ultra slow motion, let's say the word "lakh," and stop bowing. Stay in this bowed, humble, grateful position for a few seconds.

Feel your gratitude to God. Be aware that we are purposely bending our backs before God because we acknowledge God's gifts in our lives. We thank God for them.

And now, we slowly, slowly, raise our backs until we are again standing upright. Let's stand here like this for another moment or two with our eyes closed...

When you are ready, you may slowly open our eyes.

Birkat Kohanim Stylized Movements & Chant
For all ages

This is a simple and powerful exercise for Priestly Blessing found in Numbers 6:24-27 and the reader's repetition of the Amidah.

> *LEADER: God has asked us to be a holy nation, to be a nation that is a source of blessing for all people. Aaron received a three-part blessing from God and was told to bless the children of Israel using those words. Today, we are going to take the words that the children of Aaron use to bless us and we are going to use these words to bless the rest of the nations.*
>
> *Raise your hands and, if you can, shape your hands into the letter "shin" as Aaron did. This letter is the channel for Shaddai, for God's blessings to flow down through you into the world. Let's stand in a circle and face outwards. Stand quietly and think about a person or group or part of the world that you would especially like to bless today.* (Pause) *See that person or group being touched by the blessing you will transmit to them. See in your mind's eye how they receive and experience this blessing.* (Pause)
>
> *I am going to say each phrase clearly. You can repeat after me. You don't need to worry about the words. Concentrate on the message. Feel God's blessing coming to you and through you to the places you are blessing today.*

Now, word by word or phrase by phrase, clearly recite the birkat kohanim and allow the community to say it after you. Close with a hearty "Amen."

Optional: The group stands in concentric circles, with the Kohanim in the center, the Leviim in the middle circle and Yisrael on the outer circle.

יְבָרֶכְךָ ה׳ וְיִשְׁמְרֶךָ:
May God bless you and guard you

יָאֵר ה׳ פָּנָיו אֵלֶיךָ וִיחֻנֶּךָּ:
May God's presence illuminate and comfort you

יִשָּׂא ה׳ פָּנָיו אֵלֶיךָ וְיָשֵׂם לְךָ שָׁלוֹם:
May God's presence rise to you and grant you peace

Birkat Sim Shalom: A Drawing Exercise on the Letters
For all ages

There is an old Jewish tradition of creating a piece of art to focus on while we pray. The custom is to make a beautiful form out of the letters of an important word or verse from the Bible. Perhaps the most famous example is the שויתי "Shiviti" a decorated picture on paper or silver or other material of the line in the Book of Psalms 16:8, "Shiviti Adonai l'negdi tamid/I set God in front of me always." Another example is to write the letters of the name of God which is never pronounced as written (YHVH י-ה-ו-ה) in an artistic way.

Often, these simple pieces of spiritual art would be placed in a location easily seen when we pray. A "Shiviti" might be set at the place in the home where Shabbat candles are lit. Another word often used is מִזְרָח "Mizrach," "East." This would be placed on the eastern wall to remind us which direction to face when we pray. The pictures that we produce might be put on the eastern wall of our bedroom or classroom. They could also be placed anywhere in our synagogue or school as well. The main thing is that they should be visible to us, especially as we pray. Since the words we will draw or paint or sculpt are "Sim Shalom/Grant Peace" our piece of spiritual art can help us to feel an inner peacefulness as we gaze upon it in prayer or other times.

The leader should decide in advance which media the participants will use. The participants could use just one medium, say, paper with drawing materials (crayons, colored pens and pencils, cray-pa's, crayons with sparkles in them, paint, etc.). Alternatively, there could be a choice. Among the truly endless possibilities are: Clay, metal, "reverse pictures" or "black-wash pictures," textile-work, wood, montages of magazine pictures or cloth, etc.

The instructions are very simple. The words "Sim Shalom" in Hebrew should be displayed in several different styles for the participants. The participants should be shown the prayer in its context, at the beginning of the last bracha in the Amidah of Shacharit (the morning service). The explanation above regarding the history and function of this kind of ritual art should be shared. It should be stressed that they should try to encompass a feeling of Shalom in their creation as they choose the style of lettering, colors, and decorations or shading around the letters.

BIRKAT SIM SHALOM:
A DRAWING EXERCISE ON THE LETTERS

Participants should be encouraged to make the letters large and readable, at least to themselves. The goal is for their project to be an ongoing source and reminder of the most pleasant feeling of peace that they can imagine. Such a feeling comes from God. That is why we ask God in this blessing to "Sim Shalom," to "Grant Peace."

שִׂים שָׁלוֹם

שים שלום

שים שלום

שים שלום

שים שלום

שים שלום

שים שלום

שים שלום

שים שלום

שים שלום

HALLEL, KRIYAT HA-TORAH & CLOSING PRAYERS
THE DANCING HALLELUYAHS
FOR ALL AGES

Psalms, which contain references to dancing and singing for joy, are included in the daily prayers at several points and in the Hallel. Several of these Psalms lend themselves beautifully to dance interpretations. If your group is large, divide them into groupings of 3 or 4 and assign them to dance/act out various verses. They can teach them to the larger group as part of the tefilah. Psalm 118 from Hallel is especially good for this exercise.

If members of your group have musical skills and/or simple instruments, music can be added to support your dance recitations of the Psalms.

THEMATIC ALIYOT LA-TORAH
FOR ALL AGES

This is a way to deepen the experience of aliyot la-torah. Thematic aliyot personalize the Torah's message and deepen the experience of going up to draw inspiration from the Torah.

The minimum required reading for an aliyah varies a great deal by custom but a minimum of three is the shortest acceptable reading. For this exercise, scan the Torah portion that will be recited. Thematic Aliyot means that you will be calling up to the Torah any members of your community that have a special relationship with the content of that particular reading. Everyone who feels moved by that particular reading comes up and they all pronounce the blessings together. After the reading, a personalized misheberach is recited. You can start the blessing with the traditional "May the One who blessed our ancestors..." A Torah insight from that groups' aliyah is then restated within the misheberach, in the form of an inspiration or blessing. (Examples below). Close your blessing with the traditional formula "...since they have honored the Sabbath and honored the community and sought guidance from the wisdom of Torah. And let us all say Amen." Everyone is then seated and the theme for the next reading is described. People can come up for any or all of the thematic aliyot. A maximum of three readings framed in this fashion is suggested.

You will need to select verses from the Torah reading that you think will be meaningful to members of your community. As each aliyah is introduced, draw the group's attention to the verses or message you are highlighting. You will also need to spend some time understanding and encapsulating the message or blessing that you can draw from that Torah reading for the members of your community. A few moments of prayer and meditation prior to the service will be needed for you to prepare the themes and the blessings for your personalized aliyot.

SAMPLE THEMATIC ALIYAH

As an example of thematic aliyot, say, if you had called people up for the first reading of Lech Lecha. You might say that this aliyah is open to anyone who feels that they are getting ready to begin a new venture or a new phase in their lives. After the aliyah, you might ask God to bless them and guide them. Or you might pray that they remember that they are not alone on their journey. They can call on the courage and inspiration of our many ancestors who heard the small voice and began their quest.

> *ENERGY TIP: Using the opening formula of misheberach (or something similar) humbly reminds us of our chain of ancestors in whose merit we ask for guidance. The closing formula allows the community to give its blessing to the olim latorah. Blessing is, after all, the community's emotional energy directed in a specific and beneficial way.*
>
> *You will want to choose key themes from the reading in advance. This will require some intuition, open-heartedness or simply a feel for who will be there and what the issues are in their lives. We re-read Torah every year with the understanding that there is wisdom in it; we can always find some way that the text is speaking to us.*

ALEYNU BLESSING CIRCLE
FOR ALL AGES

LEADER: In the first half of the Aleynu, we thank God for giving us a special role to play in humanity. We thank God for making us so unique and so separate from all the other nations. But in the second half of the Aleynu, we pray for something quite opposite. We ask God to inspire us to bring about the time when all people will play a part in our special mission. Today we will create together our vision of that time when all people understand the unity of all creation.

Gather the group into a circle.

Let's think about the time referred to at the end of the prayer: When "God is One and God's name is Unity." What does that time look like? What will be healed? Who will stop suffering? Whose life will be better? How will we treat each other? (Pause)

Let's pray in a personal way today about what that time will be like. We pray to you, Holy One to see the time when... (Leader should open with a sample intention, such as "when every child will have enough food, when love will permeate every family and home, when there won't be diseases...")

Allow time for members of the group to articulate their blessings.

LEADER: Let's take a minute to really imagine the images we have heard today. See in your mind's eye how the world looks when it is healed in the ways we have expressed today. (Pause) *May God grant us the strength to work towards that time!*
(Sing) ***V'ne-emar, v'haya Adonai..."***

וְנֶאֱמַר. וְהָיָה ה' לְמֶלֶךְ עַל כָּל הָאָרֶץ.
בַּיּוֹם הַהוּא יִהְיֶה ה' אֶחָד וּשְׁמוֹ אֶחָד:

Shalom Dance & Chant*

For all ages
*The tune, by Rabbi Shlomo Carlebach, z"l
is included on the accompanying tape.

This Shalom chant is a nice closing exercise for various services or experiences.

> LEADER: We are going to close today with the best-known Hebrew word: Shalom. Shalom means Peace, as you know. It also means fullness or whole. Today we are going to do a movement with the word shalom that shows this meaning of wholeness.
>
> Let's stand in a circle, feet about shoulder length apart. Good. Stand right in your own center, evenly on both legs. Good. Now, when we say shalom, we are intending to include everything, heaven and earth. Let's start by bending our knees a little and scooping up from the earth and reaching up to heaven. Now for the first shalom, we will plant this fullness into the earth. With your hands still held high, slowly press this heavenly energy down towards the ground. Feel your feet firmly on the ground. Feel your strong connection to the earth and your own center. Good.
>
> For the second shalom, we are going to thank all the group that has helped us have such a nice experience today. Start again by scooping up from the earth and reaching towards heaven and now shower this shalom around our circle. Good.
>
> This time we are going to keep the shalom. We are going to put it into our own hearts. Start by scooping and then reaching up, and now pull that shalom into your own heart. Good.
> This last time, we are going to share this shalom with the rest of the

world. Scoop up energy from earth; move it up towards heaven. Now bring your hands down in front of you, facing outwards and slowly circle around, blessing the planet with peace. OR

This last time, we are going to hold on to the shalom, we are going to carry it home with us. Scoop down, and now up again. Now slowly bring your hands together and then lower them down together to the level of your heart. Feel the shalom moving through you, up and down and all around you. OR

This last time, you can repeat any movement you like. Keep the energy for yourself, or ground it or send it around the circle.

Let's do the whole dance again, first grounding the energy, then sharing it, then putting it into yourself and then doing the movement that you want to repeat.

Amen.

Optional: Add motions or do them in a different order to suit the energy and situation of your group. For example, you may want to imagine someone in your community who is ill in the center of the circle. Holding hands in front of you, use one "shalom" to bless that person.

Kavanah Before Kaddish Yatom (Mourner's Kaddish)
For all ages

An evocative poem can serve to focus the congregation on the moment of kaddish yatom: a sober moment of personal reflection for all and support for the bereaved. We have included one such poem by grief counselor, Anne Brenner.

Mourning for Peace

When we mourn, we strain our ears,
listening for the voice of the deceased--until we hear
that voice coming from our own hearts.
Mourners, we yearn to continue the conversation.
We search for the unsaid words, to resolve
the unfinished issues.

The Kaddish can take us there.
Kaddish parts the curtains and forces open
the space between the worlds, breaking open
the crevices where the voices still come through
and where all the worlds are one.
For the price of our yearning, our anger and our tears,
the Kaddish will carry us beyond the edges
of the world we know.
It takes us to a place of wholeness- of peace-
where all the polarities dissolve, where life and death,
black and white, male and female, God and not-God
merge- become one.
Adonai Ehad.
The words of the Shema become the reality of the world.

Kaddish ends exile.
It suffuses the most profane regions
with the holiness of God's name
and wrests an Amen from the place it has not yet been forthcoming, the
Amen we have been listening for for our entire lives.
That Amen sustains the world.

The Mourner's Kaddish: A Visualization of the Inner Smile

For Middle School Through Adult

The words of our tradition's central mourning prayer do not contain any reference to death or the dead. The Kaddish probably was not originally written for use as a mourner's prayer.[14] Hope for the coming of the Messianic era is hinted at early in the prayer ("v'yamlich malchutei," "and may His kingdom reign"), and this may have been the connection to comforting mourners.[13] The prayer as it stands today, however, consists mainly of repeated praises to God, Who is "l'eila mikol... tushb'chata," "beyond all... praise." This may seem to make the prayer ill-suited for meaningful use by a mourner since a mourner's naturally sad mood may prevent him or her from reciting God's praises with a full heart. Many have nevertheless experienced the healing potential of the Kaddish when the following simple visualization is suggested.

> **LEADER:** *As we recite the words of the Mourner's Kaddish, let's try to visualize something in our mind's eye. Since the words of the Kaddish consist, more than anything else, of praise to God, perhaps they are a challenge to us to thank God for our deep connection to our loved one. It may well be too difficult to bring a smile to our faces as we say the Kaddish, but an inner smile may well be possible. If anyone feels too upset over the loss of a loved one to participate in this exercise, then, by all means, do not feel that you must join in.*
>
> *As we recite the words of the Kaddish, envision a happy time with your loved one. Try right now to hold a scene of your loved one in your heart that brings you an inner smile to you. I'll pause*

---

[14] The classic work on the Kaddish is still: David de Sola Pool, <u>The Old Jewish Aramaic Prayer: The Kaddish</u> (New York: Bloch, 1964).

The Mourner's Kaddish: A Visualization of the Inner Smile

for half a minute or so to allow each of us to envision this kind of scene. (Pause).

As we say the Kaddish now, let's keep that vision of a happy time with our loved one in our consciousness...

Slowly recite the Mourner's Kaddish.

Shofarot: Listening With Intention
For all ages

In ancient times, our people used the shofar to call the community together in all sorts of situations. Each blast (or combination of sounds) communicated a different message. We know very little about what those messages were, but the shofar sound continues to be a deeply evocative moment in our worship! During the month of Elul and during the High Holiday liturgy, we listen intently to the sounds of the shofar in an effort to "wake up" to our continued development. This conversation and listening exercise allows us to listen carefully to the piercing sounds of the shofar.

Sit with your group in a circle. Have several shofarot around the circle.

Leader opens a conversation with the following questions:

תְּקִיעָה **Tekiah** is considered to be the spiritual wake up call. What does it feel like to be woken up by the alarm clock in the morning? We usually feel resistance when we first hear that buzzer in the morning. What is it about our alarm clock that helps us overcome that resistance? That's tekiyah, our call to consciousness. What is it that you are now working on? What lessons are coming to your consciousness now? What is it that you want to wake up to?

Make a list of these things.

As you listen to the sound of tekiyah, listen with these things in mind and let the sound move you towards greater awareness.

שְׁבָרִים **Shevarim**: Means broken. Where are you hurting? Where is there brokenness inside? Write some of these down. Listening to shevarim, let the sound express this inner hurt for you.

תְּרוּעָה **Teruah** is a call to action. What "really gets you going"? What gets your blood moving? What stirs you to action? Reflect on some experiences of being moved to act in a powerful way. Was it an experience of being moved by a dangerous situation? Were you moved by fear? Perhaps it was the experience of being loved or caring deeply. Listening to

Shofarot: Listening With Intention

Teruah, feel your heart beat faster, feel your blood move. Feel yourself stirred to act.

תְּקִיעָה גְדוֹלָה **Tekiyah Gedola** is the Great Cry. Each of us has something to shout out to the world, some message within us that we're anxious to communicate. What do you think this message might be? What is it that you want to shout out to the world? How might we use our brokenness and that which stirs us to action to help us bring this great cry out of us? Listening to Tekiyah Gedolah, hear it as the expression of your own great cry.

> *Listen to the call of shofar in Elul with these intentions in mind.*

Shabbat Table and Home Blessings
Hadlakat Nerot/ Lighting Candles: A Standing Meditation
For all ages

The kindling of lights marks the entry of Sabbath and holy days into a home. It is a very appropriate time to pause, reflect and receive Sabbath peace. The following is a standing meditation.

When you are ready to receive Shabbat, stand before your holiday candles. Close your eyes and stand calmly, breathing naturally. Feel the firm fullness of your feet on the floor. Rock on your feet, back and forth, 3-4 times and stand firmly again. Imagine the area at the very top of your head as an entry point into your mind. Feel the light energy pouring through you through this point. Imagine the continuation of this line which pours out of your perineum. The line continues straight through you to a point deep in the earth. Stand this way for 20 breaths. Light candles as per your custom.

בָּרוּךְ אַתָּה ה' אֱלֹהֵינוּ מֶלֶךְ הָעוֹלָם
אֲשֶׁר קִדְּשָׁנוּ בְּמִצְוֹתָיו וְצִוָּנוּ
לְהַדְלִיק נֵר שֶׁל שַׁבָּת.

The Imahot/Matriarch's Meditation
For all ages

Lighting candles has long been associated with women. We use this kavanah to draw from the images of our mothers.

Begin with the Hadlakat Nerot Standing Meditation (previous page).

Light your candles and move your arms in three sweeping motions, as if pulling the light towards your eyes. Imagine that you are pouring light into your mind and heart; and into your body; and the space around you.

Imagine the strong white desert light that shone through the tents of Sarah and of Rebecca. Feel the warmth and the light of those ancestresses. Feel the desert wind.

Revisit the women of our people who have kindled lights for centuries around the world. Touch the light of their homes, of their shabbat.

Imagine the wave of light that is spreading across the planet; now in this moment that is the moment of your kindling. That wave is the peace of Sabbath spreading out over the planet, time-zone by time-zone as the homes of Israel kindle the light.

Recite or sing the blessing in your customary fashion.

How to Give a Blessing
For high school through adults

In the moments after lighting candles, it is customary to bless our loved ones. The following is a formula for giving blessings.

1. Concentrate on the person you are blessing. Concentrate on your love for that person. Imagine God's חֶסֶד /chesed/free-flowing love as it moves through the universe. For this moment, you can be a channel for that חֶסֶד /chesed.
2. Think about any challenges being faced by that person. What is their special need at this time? Often our deepest needs are quite simple: To feel loved, hopeful and so on. Open yourself to be a humble vessel for whatever blessings this person may need at this time. Think of the message you would like to give this person at this time. Condense the message into one strong sentence.
3. Here's the magic part: Using your feeling of חֶסֶד /chesed as the wire – send the message to that person. In a moment, "see" them understanding the message, in your mind's eye.

Kiddush for Shabbat Evening: A Guided Meditation on Releasing*

FOR ALL AGES
*This guided meditation is included on the accompanying tape

Before we personally accept the Shabbat in our home by reciting the Kiddush over the wine on Friday night, we would do well to make an inner transformation from the busy pace of the workweek to the relaxed pace of Shabbat. The Talmud and Midrash emphasize in several places that our model in this is God.[15] The Torah teaches us (Exodus 20:9) that: "Six days we shall labor and do *all* our work." The Torah is hinting that on Friday, we assume the mind-set that *all* our work is finished. The goal of this exercise is to help us let go of the tensions of getting things done, and to feel the release that comes with Shabbat rest. With this outlook, reciting the Kiddush over the wine can become a true spiritual beginning of the Shabbat mind-set.

Use one of the relaxation exercises on pages 28-33 to focus and relax participants.

> *LEADER:* **Let us sit comfortably and gently close our eyes. Here in our home, (or "in our synagogue") we are about to make the transition from the workweek to Shabbat. To do that, we will want to bring closure to the week, which is concluding tonight, according to the Jewish calendar.**
>
> **I am going to ask to scan the week's activities and moods. There may have been several lows and several highs for each of us this week. I am going to ask you to revisit briefly one low point and one high point of the week.**
>
> **I'd like us to begin with the low point.**

---

[15] The Talmud, on Shabbat 119b says that when a person recites the Kiddush on Friday night, quoting the biblical verses which describes God resting on the first Shabbat, it is as if that person is a partner with God in creation.

Kiddush for Shabbat Evening: A Guided Meditation on Releasing

> *Take a moment or two to think back over the week, from this past Sunday until this evening, to identify one difficult point for ourselves. It may have to do with work or school or with a friend or family member, or just some issue that is yours alone. Try to distinguish such an event from this past week.*

Give the group a moment or two to focus on a low point.

> *Once you have a low point of our week in focus, try to see the scene clearly. Although it may be a bit painful, try to replay very briefly the scene in your mind's eye.*

Again, give a moment or two.

> *Now, let's close the scene. It is over. Whatever it was, whatever difficulties it caused, whatever hurt may have accompanied it, it is over. The week is ending. Take in a cleansing deep breath... And release it; see it rise off in your mind like a helium balloon. This part of our week is over.*

> *Now, take a moment or two to think back over the week, from this past Sunday until this evening, to identify one high point, one joyful time for yourself, one moment of success and accomplishment. Again, it may come from a variety of settings from your life this week. It may have to do with others, or it may have occurred when you were by yourself. Try to focus in on such a time.*

Give the group a moment or two to focus on a high point.

> *Once you have a high point of our week in focus, try to see the scene clearly.*

> *Very briefly replay the scene in your mind's eye.*

Again, give a moment or two.

Kiddush for Shabbat Evening: A Guided Meditation on Releasing

Now, with a smile of thanks for that time of happiness let us close this scene, too. The week is ending. Take in a cleansing deep breath... And release it. This part of our week is over as well.

It is time to relax that part of ourselves that seeks to accomplish, to create, to make or do or build. It is time to accept that very special gift from God that is a full day to just be. When we recite the Kiddush and drink the wine in a moment, it will truly be the opening ritual of a day of rest. May we accept it fully, joyfully, and thankfully.

When you are ready, you may open our eyes.

Ha-motzi, The Mystery in the Wheat: An "Eating" Exercise
For all ages

This is an exercise designed to motivate participants to think about the origin of our food, and God's role in bringing food to our table. Needed: Bread slices and wheatberries – the part of the wheat plant that is ground into flour. Wheatberries are available at many Health Food stores. Paper napkins or plates are suggested as well. It might be a good idea if a variety of bread that is tasty even when eaten by itself is selected (such as honey-wheat bread). You may also want to provide honey or jam to make the bread more appetizing to the participants.

There are two parts to this exercise: A brief question and answer session on the origin of our bread and a spiritually conscious eating of bread.

A Brief Question and Answer Session on the Origin of our bread.

Each participant should be provided with a piece of bread and several wheatberries on a paper napkin or plate.

The leader should tell the participants that the wheatberries are the "fruit" or seeds of the wheat plant, that they grow on the long stalks of wheat, and that it is from these wheatberries that flour for bread is made.

The leader should then ask the participants to do the following:

1. List on a piece of paper all of the stages of the preparation of this bread that you can think of from its origin to a piece of bread. Think of all the places the wheat and then the flour and then the bread had to travel in order to get to us. List these places on your paper. (The list should include: Supermarket or bakery where it was bought, bakery where it was baked, mill where the wheatberries were ground into flour, farm where the wheat stalks were grown, and all the delivery vehicles used as well.)

Ha-motzi, The Mystery in the Wheat: An "Eating" Exercise

Ask individual participants to volunteer stages. Put these on the board.
2. Imagine the wheatberries (which are seeds of the wheat plant) in the ground on the farm. What makes these wheatberries grow into wheat plants? (Proper sunlight and warmth, water, and nutrients in the soil).
3. Imagine the wheatberries in the ground on the farm again. Why is it that the wheat will grow when there is enough sunlight, warmth, water and nutrients in the soil?

I don't want us to answer this question, because nobody knows the answer. It is a mystery. Thousands of years ago, human beings discovered, probably by accident, that seeds that we plant will grow if there is enough sun and water. Until then, human beings ate whatever grew by itself. And even though it is now thousands of years later, we still can't answer the "why" question: "Why will the plant grow when there is enough sun and water." It is one of those mysteries that makes us think that God takes care of us. It is because of this mystery that whenever we are about to eat bread, we thank God. We thank God in the words of the Hamotzi. This blessing thanks God "Hamotzi lechem min ha'aretz," "Who brings forth bread from the earth." It isn't that we understand how God does this. It is still a mystery. But it is such a mystery – even though we rarely think about it -- that we feel God is involved. It is a challenge to us to think of the mystery and God, and to thank God each time we eat bread.

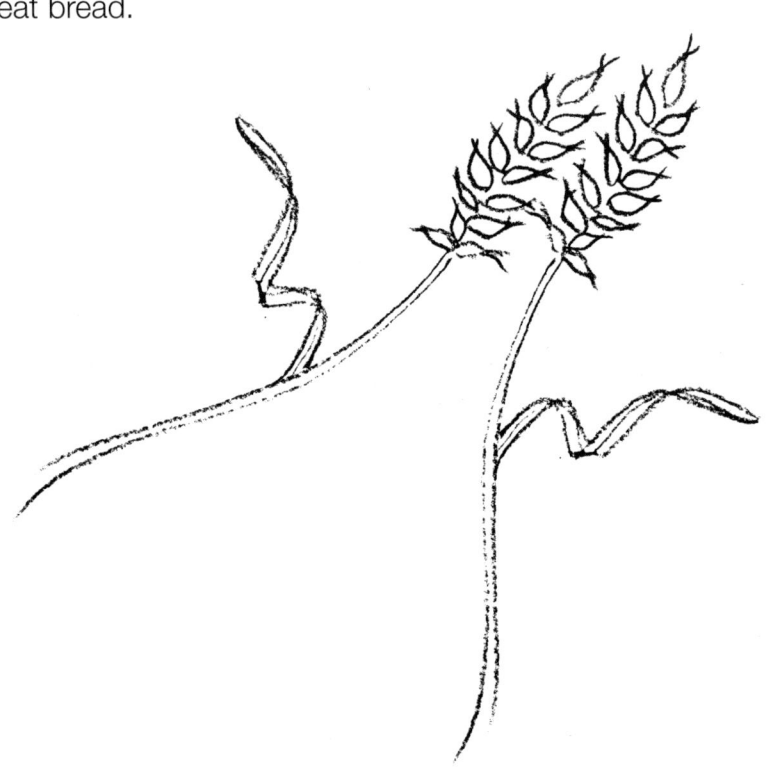

Ha-motzi, The Mystery in the Wheat: An "Eating" Exercise

A Spiritually-Conscious Eating of Bread.

Use one of the relaxation exercises from pages 28-33.

> *LEADER: We are going to recite the Ha-motzi very slowly together and then we are going to eat the bread, but very slowly. Let's do an unusual thing as we eat: Every time we bring our teeth together to chew, -- every time! -- let's think about another stage that the wheat had to go through in order to reach us. That will be slow chewing indeed! Between each chew, count to five slowly to yourself to really give time to think about each stage between seed in the ground and bread in our hands. Look at the list of stages on the board or on your papers. It is ok to go back and think about the same stages more than once. In fact, it makes sense to think about each stage several times over.*
>
> *So. Let's recite the Ha-motzi very slowly together:*
>
> בָּרוּךְ אַתָּה ה' אֱלֹהֵינוּ מֶלֶךְ הָעוֹלָם הַמּוֹצִיא לֶחֶם מִן הָאָרֶץ:
>
> *Baruch Atah Adonai Elohaynu Melech Ha-olam
> Ha-motzi Lechem Min Ha-aretz.*
>
> *Now, let's slow down our chewing! Chew once, and imagine one stage each time we chew, and then count to five slowly, chew again, and imagine another stage.*

Short Kavanah before Birkat Ha-mazon
For all ages

The Birkat Ha-mazon, the blessing after meals, is a four-part prayer thanking God for many gifts associated with food and with the greater goals of humanity. Each of the blessings has distinctive themes: 1) sustenance of every living thing; 2) the land of Israel and her produce; 3) the rebuilding of Jerusalem and 4) the good things God does for us. The theme of the conclusion is the coming of the Messiah, with the return of all the Jews to the land of Israel, and to peace

Food keeps us alive and we are alive for a reason. Our eating and then thanking is a reciprocal act: God gives us food and we in turn promise to live the way God wants us to live. We promise to use the strength that comes from each and every meal to do good works. A simple meditation before the birkat ha-mazon can help us be more mindful of that promise!

One of the relaxation exercises can be used here.

> *LEADER: Before we recite the birkat ha-mazon, we are going to take a moment to think about our food, to think about the energy we get from it and to remember what we might to with that energy.*
>
> *Everyone please close your eyes for a moment. Sit up a little straighter. Try to pay attention to your body with your eyes closed. Pay attention to the food that has just entered your body. You are already beginning the process of changing this meal into strength and energy.*
>
> *Imagine for a moment, the journey that the food of this meal had to make in order to get to us today. Where did it begin? As grains or vegetables or fruit growing in the soil, with the sun shining on it and the rain watering it. Imagine the journey as the food moves from the farm and other places to the factory to be baked or cooked or put into packages. Then to the market and to your*

home or your school. Imagine the many hands and all the work that went into bringing this meal to your plate.

Let's pause for a moment to accept onto our bodies the kindness of God, the energy of the soil and rain and sun and all the beings which brought this nourishment to us (Pause for 10 seconds or so) *And now, let's accept the responsibility to raise up the energy of this food. Imagine what mitzvot we can perform with this life-energy. Imagine what kind word we can say. Imagine what tzedakah we can give. What act of chesed/kindness will be fueled by this food? Remember, at this moment, that we are endlessly receiving and giving. In gratitude, we recite Birkat Hamazon...*

La'asok B'Divrei Torah: To "Soak" Up the Words of the Torah - At the Beginning of a Study Session
For all ages

While deeds of kindness form the most valued kind of activity according to tradition, study and worship are close runners-up. And these two are tied together in an interesting way: At the beginning of the Siddur, right at the start of Shacharit, the morning service, there is a "mini" learning session, which includes some excerpts from the holy books... on the subject of deeds of kindness. Our Sages acknowledged that all study and all knowledge – from any source - can lead us to an awareness of God, because God is the Source of all. However, the overtly spiritual nature of Torah may bring a more directly spiritual study experience. Therefore, introducing these passages is a bracha that can help us to focus on the spiritual nature of studying Torah. This meditation is meant as a preface to that bracha, and can be used, along with the bracha itself, to begin a Jewish class or study session. If this meditation is used often, the first, introductory, paragraph may be skipped. Proceed directly to the meditation and to the bracha. You may want to begin with a relaxation exercise.

> *LEADER: We are about to begin Torah study. We have all come to this space, this room, from different places today. Our journey today began at home, continued to this building, and, winding around through the corridors and other rooms here, ended in this room, in the specific place where we are now sitting. When we daven or study Torah, our personal space is transformed into what our tradition calls the "arba amot shel tefilah," the "four square feet of prayer." Some people living today call it "sacred space." Sacred space is holy space, a place at which each of us, as an individual, does holy things. We study or daven at our seats*

La'asok B'Divrei Torah: To "Soak" Up the Words of the Torah - At the Beginning of a Study Session

often, and this can cause us to lose sight of the holiness of our Torah study. It is for that reason that the tradition has us recite a bracha before each time we begin study, to remind us that when we learn something new, we are learning something about God. And so, just before we recite the bracha, Birkat La'asok B'Divrei Torah, I'll ask us לְכַוֵּון אֶת לִבֵּנוּ *lechavven et lebeinu, to direct our hearts, and to concentrate on the transformation of the space around us into sacred space.*

Close your eyes for a moment or two. In your mind, trace your journey from your home this morning to the building we are now in, and from the entrance to the building, to this room. (Pause for about half a minute). *Good. Continue to keep your eyes closed for another moment or two. Now imagine, yourself sitting where you are right now.* (Pause for about 5 seconds). *Now, imagine yourself opening a Sefer Torah, a scroll of the Torah, right in front of you. As you open the scroll and look inside, imagine that you are able to see beyond the words and the letters, to deep, true and important lessons that God has taught our prophets and sages about life. Concentrate on that scene.* (Pause for about 15 seconds).

Now, let's thank God for the experience of sacred space and Torah study through the words of the bracha. Let's recite it together now, very slowly, in a soft and calm voice:

בָּרוּךְ אַתָּה ה' אֱלֹהֵינוּ מֶלֶךְ הָעוֹלָם.
אֲשֶׁר קִדְּשָׁנוּ בְּמִצְוֹתָיו וְצִוָּנוּ לַעֲסוֹק בְּדִבְרֵי תוֹרָה

Baruch Atah Adonai Elohaynu Melech Ha-olam Asher Kid'shanu Bemitzvotav Vetzivanu La'asok B'divrei Torah.

Praised are You, Adonai our God, Cosmic Ruler, Who has made us holy through the mitzvot and Who has given us the mitzvah to study words of Torah.

NEW BLESSINGS
FOR MIDDLE SCHOOL THROUGH ADULT

Jews are enjoined to bless 100 times a day. If we perform the three daily services and bless before and after meals, we come pretty close to our 100. There is no prohibition, however, to saying free-form personal blessings of thanks and appreciation. The act of turning our heart towards heaven at any number of special moments during the day is an elevating practice and a very good habit for children and adults. This exercise is intended to help our learners grasp the difficult process of creating liturgy.

Maimonides taught us that the blessing formula set "by the sages" is preferable but we may bless in any language that is moving for us. The required formula for a blessing is to 1) call on God by name; 2) to name God's relationship to our world; and 3) to name the specific topic of our blessing. Traditional blessings are structured this way:

1. "Blessed are You" is the first section Maimonides describes; called *shem*/naming our God;
2. "Our God and Ruler of the Universe" is called *malkhut*/Kingship by Maimonides, naming God's relationship to the world (part 2);
3. The last part of the blessing (Who creates food of the vine, for example) names the specific topic, variously praises, or thanksgiving or requests for help.

In this exercise, we suggest a "mix and match" approach to creating blessings that are meaningful for you and your students. You may want to begin by doing one of the lesson plans on God's many names. (See pages 182-189)

Talk to your students about moments that stand out for them in the course of a day. You may want to pepper the conversation with a few suggestions, such as:

Finishing a really interesting book
Doing well on a test that you were anxious about
Making up with parents and/or friends after an argument
Noticing signs of maturity and growth on your part
Making a hard decision.

Write a few of these blessing opportunities on the board. Are there any

New Blessings

God-names (from your previous exercises) that would match particularly well with the ideas your group has generated? Why is that name or aspect of God especially suitable for that given blessing opportunity?

This conversation has helped you create parts one and two of the blessing schema: 1) How we name or call upon God; and 2) What aspect of God touches us in this situation. To finish the "blessing" we simply restate our current situation in a more poetic fashion.

1. Shem/Naming God:
Some suggestions for the first section include (and are not limitted to):
We Praise You, God of All
We turn our hearts to You
Let us give thanks to our God
Let us bless the Source
We are grateful to the Source of Life

2. Malchut/Kingship:
This second section of the prayer formula states God's relationship with the world:
Source of Life
Creator of all
God of all the worlds
Sustainer of all the worlds
Protector of the earth

3. The blessing ocassion
To finish the blessing, we mix and match parts one and two with the specific moment of appreciation.
So, for example, if I have just finished a wonderful book, I may close it and hold it to me and say: "We thank you Source of Wisdom, who blesses us with understanding and has given us the words to share insight and inspiration with each other."
Or perhaps I just settled an argument with my friend: We are grateful to You, Wellspring of Peace, Who inspires us to weave our conflicts into deeper harmonies.
If you are sending a child off to camp or college (or if you are a young person going off for the first time) you might say: We turn our hearts to You, Sustainer of all life, who guides our steps through these stages of life.

Practice creating and using personal blessings. See the lesson on God's Names page 186 as a supplement or precursor.

THE SHIELD: KAVANAH FOR "THE HELPING PROFESSIONAL"
FOR MIDDLE SCHOOL THROUGH ADULT

Kavanah/intention is the simplest Hebrew way to refer to the whole area of mindful attention. There are specific kavanot worked into much Jewish liturgy - for example, the phrase "Open up my lips O God that I may sing your praises" is a kavanah appended to the first paragraph of the Amidah. But kavanah in general means the practice of concentrating on the action before and as you perform it.

THE SHIELD

This practice is designed for teachers, therapists, guides; and other helping professionals.

Before meeting with a client or group, sit or stand on a comfortable way. Pull your attention inward, to yourself, to your body. Visualize a point in your belly about an inch below the navel and an inch inward. Breathe to that point; visualize warmth and energy gathering at that point. Let it fill. A white light fills your belly now and rises upward through your body. Visualize the white light spreading up and through each organ and limb. Finally the energy has filled your upper body and comes emanating out of the top of your head, now cascading down around you in a swirl. An oval forms all around you and comes together under your feet. The light enters your lower body and rises to meet in the belly again. Imagine that an oval shield of fine light is circling around your body. Feel the protection of that light. Only constructive energy can come in through the shield.

Quiet your mind a bit and open your imagination to the experience you are going to have with this person or class. Let the various images flow through your mind's eye. Open yourself to give and receive in the most loving possible way. Imagine the best possible outcome for this session or class. In your own words, offer yourself as a vessel for God's love and wisdom, whatever that expression may be.

STORIES

A story creates a world. Tefilah, too is like a world we want to create and enter. In sharing spiritual exercises with youngsters, we have found the tools of stories to be key aids to creating a cohesive attentiveness in a group. Included are just a few mashalim/parables and poignant stories that help amplify some of the themes of tefilah. We have provided some suggested moments for inserting these stories into the service.

THE EARTH IS ALIVE: A CAMP FIRE STORY

Read to the group:

The earth is alive. She breathes. She has a respiratory system. The respiratory system of the earth is the trees, the quivering leaves of the planet. The wind that sweeps across the planet, touching and moving everything is the breath of the earth. The leaves of the earth take in the gasses that we exhale. They release their oxygen, which all animals need for life. Our lungs are the lungs of the earth. The earth is alive and she breathes. *(Pause)*

The earth is alive and she has a circulatory system. The rains of the planet, and the rivers, the streams and the oceans, the clouds and the reservoirs, the blood in our veins and the fluid in all living systems: This is the circulatory system of the earth. *(Pause)*

The earth is alive and she digests. The worms of the soil and the bacteria in our guts are the digestive tract of the earth. The soil and the vegetation, the humus and the excrement of all life, this is the digestive system of the earth.

The earth is alive. After eons and eons, the earth has begun to be aware of herself. The earth is alive and she thinks. We, our minds, we are the thought of the earth.

This story works well as a campfire story or a teaching around Tu B'shevat.

The Mountain

Once upon a time, a woman had a strong desire to climb the mountain. She was captivated by the sheer height and beauty of the mountain! She wished for the strength that would be required to climb it! Nothing could appeal to her more.

She set about gathering the equipment. She acquired the right shoes and all the provisions she'd need. And because of her training in Judaism, she filled her backpack with Torah & mitzvot; she had been told that these tools prepared one for everything.

She began her climb. At first, the way was dark. The view was crowded by trees. Her legs ached at the end of each day and her backpack seemed to weigh a ton. Self-doubt crossed her mind and all sense of progress was invisible. But she soothed herself with the comforting thought that at least she was trying. In all her long days, she never saw another soul on the trail. With a bit of arrogance and a bit of self-satisfaction, she struggled with her physical discomfort by judging herself superior to any and all who hadn't even made the attempt.

After a while, she ascended to a level where the woods began to thin. Her legs were stronger now. She woke to welcome the climb and the challenge ahead. Each day, she felt her strength and her progress. She was in a constant state of pleasure, physical and emotional. Her burdens seemed light and her progress profound. Quite the opposite of her emotional state in the early stages of the climb, she often wished a little wish that she was not so alone. Her arrogance was replaced by a delicious sort of yearning: If only everyone could have this pleasure! And strangely enough, just at that point, she began to have glimpses now and then of other travelers. She noticed that not all the climbers were Jews, they were, in fact, a varied lot. She was surprised at first. She thought that only the provisions of the Jewish faith would suffice for this climb. "What do you know?" she would muse, "Hindus climb and humanists and..."

Finally at the top, she looked down and could see the mountain all around. From that elevation, she could barely discern where her particular path had begun. Every single path led all the way to the top, for every climber that could persevere.

> *This story compliments the intent of the Aleynu. The first paragraph of the Aleynu is quite ethnocentric; the second paragraph is more universalistic. This story could also be told early in the service as we take on the mitzvah to love our fellow as ourselves.*

The Bartender and the Rebbe

Once there was a young man who had a rebbe. Now a rebbe is like a rabbi, but a little different. A rebbe is a soul teacher. You can ask a rabbi what is kosher to put in your mouth, but ask a rebbe what is kosher to put in your heart! The student loved his rebbe very much. He felt as though his rebbe could look right into his soul and read it like a book. He felt as if his rebbe's words could heal him and teach him all at once.

If you have such a person in your life, you want to be with him as often as possible. And so it was that the student went to see his rebbe. Once, on his way to visit, the student had a strange experience at a local tavern. He had stopped at the bar to have a meal and a rest; and there he noticed something strange. The bartender, the simple bartender, had the same power as the rebbe to give a blessing! The student watched as person after person came to the bartender. Each time, the bartender spoke to the person as if he was reading from the scroll of their heart. Each time, he would say exactly the problem and exactly the fixing for that person's soul. His words were like medicine.

The student hurried to his rebbe and told what he had seen at the bar. Now the rebbe, always eager to learn from a new master, headed straight for the bar. There he saw exactly what the student had seen: the bartender was a real blesser!

The rebbe asked modestly if the bartender could spare him a moment, "one rebbe to another." Of course, the bartender was a little confused. Why would the rebbe refer to him as a fellow rebbe? But enjoying the attention and not wishing to offend the sage, the bartender went off to the side for a chat with the rebbe.

"Are you one of the secret Tzaddikim, one of the holy hidden teachers?" asked the rebbe, staring probingly into the simple man's eyes. "A secret tzaddik?" mused the bartender, "I'm afraid I don't know what you mean." The rebbe could see that the bartender was telling the truth. He was a gruff man, not refined at all. He showed no sign of a Torah education. If he was one of the hidden righteous ones, he was well-hidden, indeed. But still, those blessings! Where could a power like that come from?

The Bartender and the Rebbe

"Then tell me your mitzvah," the rebbe continued. "You must have done some great mitzvah and your special power is your reward." Now the bartender was plainly confused. "I really have no idea what you're talking about. I have no great mitzvah and no special power that I know of!" he replied.

The rebbe pondered and then shared his confusion with the simple man. "How is it that you come by the power to bless?" the rebbe blurted out. "You see so clearly, right to the wound on the heart of the soul, and then your blessings, so sweet, so powerful. How did you learn how to do that?"

"Oh that!" replied the bartender, brightening up. He finally had a question to which he knew the answer!

"Rebbe," he said, "holy teacher, you don't know me well at all, but Oy! Have I got a temper! The worst, really. Everyone who would come into my bar I found terribly annoying. In this one I saw arrogance and in that one so much shame. Every single person, sooner or later, was very grating on me. And I couldn't control myself either. I blurted it out. 'Oh, you're such an arrogant one. You think you're the only one here with a head on your shoulders?' or I would say: 'You're so shy! Do you think the world will fall apart if you say what you think one time?'

"As you can imagine, holy rebbe, I wasn't much fun to be around. And it wasn't too good for business either! Actually, we were starving. My wife begged me to take in a partner, to talk to the customers, so I wouldn't chase them all away. But it was no use. No human being could take the sharpness of my tongue.

I was really at my end. We were so hungry and no help in sight. I finally had an idea. No human being could be my partner, but the Kadosh Baruch Hu, God Himself, why would God be offended by the likes of me? I prayed the deepest prayer and asked God to be my business partner. At first, I offered God fifty-fifty; but God is God after all. We settled on 49-51. 51 percent goes straight to the beggars and tzedakah collectors.

I still get so annoyed by all the irritating traits of everyone I see. I even still blurt it out. But ever since that day until now, my partner steps in and tells me what else to say. So I see the hurt and God gives the medicine. Pretty good partnership, eh?

And good for business, too!"

> *This is a lovely story to tell any time you want to evoke our ability to be blessers and helpers: before a misheberach, at the start of the service or as a closing message.*

The Hopi and the Hasid

If you're a really great Rebbe, who teaches you? Of course, Ha-kadosh Baruch Hu, God personally, but let's face it. Sometimes you need human colleagues and friends too!

Sometimes the really big teachers of the religions of the world get together and teach each other. This is the story of something that took place at such a gathering of world teachers.

It happened in New Mexico. The month was Elul, hot, in the summer; a time when Jewish people are blowing the shofar every morning. We do it as a sort of "wake up" call. The shofar blast is very loud. You can't sleep through it. So we blow the shofar in the month before the high holidays. We want to wake ourselves up so we can be ready to face God on the high holidays.

Now our friend and teacher Reb Zalman was at the conference of the highest teachers of every faith and he had to blow the shofar first thing in the morning. This wouldn't be too polite in a hotel. But this was in New Mexico. It's hot there and it doesn't rain too much. All of the roofs in New Mexico are flat. Most are like open porches. The roof of this hotel was like a big sun deck, so Reb Zalman went up there to daven.

The first thing Reb Zalman sees on the roof is a ...Hopi medicine man. In the Native American traditions, the power that we call "soul" is called "medicine" so a soul teacher of the Hopis is called a medicine man.

The two men glanced at each other; they greeted each other just with their eyes. Reb Zalman has the custom of not speaking any words in the morning until he has spoken with Ha-kadosh Baruch Hu. It seems that the Hopi man had the same idea, so both of them just had a little look at each other and each one started to pray.

Reb Zalman took out his tallit. He waved it open and wrapped himself in it. He made his blessing and put the tallit down around his shoulders. From the corner of his eye, Reb Zalman saw the Hopi man also with a big square cloth, also shaking it open, then slowly the Hopi lowered the cloth onto the ground and sat down on it. Both men were making their praying area with a special cloth.

Next Reb Zalman took out his tefilin. He wrapped them and prayed and wrapped them and prayed. But he also looked at the Hopi. The Medicine man had taken out a pouch and removed from it a single strand of leather. This leather he carefully placed around his shoulders in the way that Reb Zalman had put on his tallit! Curious!

Each man started to pray. Reb Zalman chanted and swayed. The Hopi teacher chanted and swayed. If you didn't know Hebrew and you didn't know the Hopi language, it probably sounded pretty similar.

When the prayers were over, Reb Zalman took out his shofar and, believe it or not, the Hopi man took out a horn of a calf. Now Jewish people never use the horn of a calf for a shofar. The worst sin the Jewish people ever did was to make a golden calf while Moses was talking and talking to God on Mount Sinai. When you pray, the last thing you want to do is to remind God of the worst sin ever. But of course, any kind of animal horn can be hollowed out to make an instrument and this Hopi had the horn of a calf.

It was too much. The men approached each other and started to talk about their special objects. Reb Zalman asked about the horn. The Hopi wanted to know if the ties on the tallit had a special message. Each man learned about the other, and in a way, about themselves by talking to the other teacher.

The way I heard the story is that all of a sudden, they stopped talking and they hugged. Here was a Hopi from the hills of southwestern America and a Hasid from the forests of Eastern Europe. And here they were together, so close in their practice, so similar. In the words of the Hopi, the Great Spirit guided them both. In the words of Reb Zalman's tradition: God is One.

> *This is a great story to tell before the community dons tallit and tefilin. It speaks to the universality of these seemingly arcane practices. It is also a fine story to tell in Elul or Tishrei to review some of the practices of that season.*

LESSON PLANS

There are lesson plans elsewhere in the book, located near specific prayers and blessings. See the Outline According to Technique on page 18 for a full listing. Most of these address the conceptual framework or theological lessons that are of more general interest..

THE FOUR WORLDS
For post-bar/bat mitzvah ages

Note: This lesson plan can be an essential introduction for any prayer experience or for a group discussion about spirituality and the purpose of prayer.

> *LEADER: Today, we are going to discuss a hasidic idea for describing human nature. You don't need to agree with it or disagree, just think about it. See if it helps you describe experiences that you have had. It's called the theory of the Four Worlds.*
>
> *According to the theory, humans have four centers or four layers to their being, almost like four minds or four ways of experiencing things.*
>
> *We have bodies. This is called the world of עֲשִׂיָּה Assiyah, the world of Action. We can do things. We can learn to play golf and swim. We can effect people by touching them. This world is said to be energized through our liver, the kaved, and the largest internal organ with over 500 functions.*
>
> *If we just "do things" in Assiyah, we aren't paying attention or putting our passion into it. The emotional energy we expend is said to be the world of יְצִירָה Yeztirah, of animation or Feeling. Life is very different in the world of feeling. "Vibes" aren't exactly*

physical, but in a way, they are. "Feelings" are "embodied" as glances, body language, blood chemistry, eye contact and so on. This is our Yetzirah body, our emotional body. How we learn in Yetzirah is different from how we learn in Assiyah. Yetzirah lessons are often lessons we teach ourselves: about coping with sadness or stress, fear or joy. Feelings can seem overwhelming, disorganized, like the feelings of grief. Probably our educational systems do the poorest job of educating us in feelings.

Optional discussion about experiencing emotional lessons. A good activity is a "Whip" to finish the sentence "One of the hardest things I ever learned was…"

So the second world is the world of feelings. In symbolic language, we usually say that water represents feelings and earth or rocks represent Assiyah, practical action. Our feeling body does largely express itself through our "water" system, our circulatory system!

Now, we come to the mental world, centering in our brain, of course. Ah, the mind! The mind is the most complex physical organ. So many kinds of activity work through the mind: Memory, Computation, Associations, Comparisons, Contemplation, Translation, Dreams. The brain is a very pliable organ; we can develop it more and more. Brain researchers say that there are 15 billion possible neural connections for every moment our brain functions!

In symbolic language, we say that the mental world is represented by air. Air defines the space between things. Similarly, one of the most important functions of our mind is to help us distinguish and evaluate. In Hebrew, this realm of thoughts is called בְּרִיאָה *Briyah/Conceptualization.*

Briyah is a very subtle world, but thoughts do have power and even a physical manifestation. Thoughts occupy the space of our synapses, our neural network.

So, we have body, heart, and mind. We have one more world and no more body parts! Soul, or spirit, the world of אֲצִילוּת *Aztilut is the Fourth World. Atzilut literally means Nearness. Atzilut or Spirit is much too large to fit into your body. In Hassidic language, we say that the lower three worlds can be a container for the Fourth World, the spirit.*

This is a very simple definition of a spiritual experience. When your body, heart and mind are doing the same thing: That's a spiritual experience.

We can all think of times when we acted in the world of Assiyah/Action without really paying attention: Going through the motions. There are lots of times when our body heart and mind are not in alignment at all. We may feel pressured into doing something. We may have a strong feeling to do something (or avoid doing something!) but other pressures – our appetites or social pressures - prevent us from acting.

Give examples from your lives about feeling "in alignment" or "out of alignment"

Leader may need to give some examples from his/her own life to get the ball rolling

LEADER: So most of us described "alignment" as moments when we felt centered, confident and energized. We might say that prayer is essentially our way of practicing being in alignment. When we pray, we take an idea and say it, think it, feel it. When we really pray, in all four worlds, we are infused with spirit. This spiritual energy is the fuel we use to go out in the world and live out the ideals we pray about.

The Four Worlds

"Today, we are going to try to daven in all four worlds…"

NEARNESS/SPIRIT	אֲצִילוּת	ATZILUT
Thought	בְּרִיאָה	Briyah
Feelings	יְצִירָה	Yetzirah
Action	עֲשִׂיָה	Assiyah

Notnim Reshut Discussion; Group Dynamics in Prayer
FOR OLDER ELEMENTARY AGES THROUGH ADULTS

LEADER: There is a very strange passage in the blessing before the morning Shema. There is a description of angels. And the angels are having a conversation. They are giving each other permission to praise God. We probably have a variety of beliefs about angels in this room (Optional discussion on angels). *But any traditional understanding of angels has the idea that angels are servants of God. They do what they're told! Yet this prayer tells us that the angels give each other permission to praise God.*

What does it mean to give each other permission to do things? We have all had experience with groups. How do groups "give permission?" Is it important to have the group's permission to do certain things? What kinds of activities are sensitive to group agreement? What happens when a group isn't in agreement? (Note: Feeling part of a group is very important to teenagers. Help them use this discussion to see how this issue of permission and group agreement effects them)

Now, the prayer says something interesting: All the angels feel loved by each other. All the angels feel clear about what they are doing. All the angels feel strong and capable AND they each have each other's permission to sing and praise. Are there times that you have felt loved in a group? Clear about your purpose? Strong and capable?

So some of us have had strong experiences with a group. Now, have any of us had times when we felt a spiritual impulse: a great feeling of gratefulness or relief? A great feeling of yearning or closeness to God? A strong experience of any of the other feelings recorded in the siddur? Were those experiences in a group or alone? What would it be like for a group to work together to express these kinds of feelings? How can a group give (or withhold) permission for this kind of activity?

When we daven together in the weeks ahead, I am going to ask you to give your permission to the group, to comfort the mourners around the kaddish or to pray for healing around the misheberakh or to feel all connected together around the Shema. We'll see if our group energy adds to each one's personal experience.

> *Move into a tefilah or exercise. After the experience, you can revisit the idea of "permission and agreement."*

God, The Writing Project
For middle elementary school students

This writing exercise is intended to help young people expand and experience a God concept. Each participant has several small cards. The word "God" is written in the middle of the first card. In standard "web" fashion, associated words are written in spokes coming off of the central word. Students select one word from the outer web and that word goes into the middle position on their second card. People free-associate on their second word until that web is full and then select one word from the second web to serve as the center of their third and final card.

Discuss with the group where they all have arrived starting from the first word "God." Most kids will have far-ranging items on their cards (gerbil is common...) but they will be able to explain to the group how they arrive there from "God."

The last part of the exercise is to write a psalm or poem using 6 or so words from their various cards. You can challenge them to use only "God" and the words from the third card. Or let them chose the nouns they wish to select. You can determine the shape of the poem (acrostic, haiku, repeating refrain, etc) or let the student write in free form.

Incorporate their poems into group tefilah.

Names of God: A Lesson Plan

In a day and age where most kings are ceremonial positions, to call God the King of Kings does not carry the weight and power it once did. On the other hand, in the century of particle physics, we understand the profound mystery of light. To name God as Yotzer Or/Generator of Light tickles us at the edge of our consciousness. It is a name that speaks to us of unfathomable mystery and power.

The names of God are innumerable. Certain names are associated with particular moments in history. The God who came to Moses, the freer of slaves, gave the name: I will become what I will become. Some names are associated with certain moments in a lifetime. When comforting mourners, we call God HaMakom/The Place. Sometimes we name God אֱלֹהֵינוּ as our collective God; other ways of calling God are more personal, and singular.

Since our relationship with God is at the heart of prayer, the nature of our conceptions about God plays a vital role in our willingness to pray! We may not be very comfortable with the images of God we have seen or we may not have thought very deeply about those conceptions.

Below is a long list of names, appellations and descriptions of God. They are gathered from the Siddur and other Jewish writings. The list is not complete, but it is comprehensive.

Find a quiet place and take from this list those names that describe how you believe in God. Your list does not need to be long, just sincere. Share your preferences with others in the group.

Names of God

1. Adonai/My Lord .... אֲדוֹנָי
2. King .... מֶלֶךְ
3. Lord .... אָדוֹן
4. Creator of Light .... יוֹצֵר אוֹר
5. The Divinity .... הָאֱלֹהִים
6. The Fear of Isaac .... פַּחַד יִצְחָק
7. Healer of All Life .... רוֹפֵא כָל בָּשָׂר
8. The Most High .... אֵל עֶלְיוֹן
9. Everlasting God .... אֱלֹהֵי עוֹלָמִים
10. God Almighty .... אֵל שַׁדַּי
11. Keeper of the Covenant .... זוֹכֵר הַבְּרִית
12. Living God Who Sees Me .... אֵל חַי רוֹאִי
13. Redeemer .... גּוֹאֵל
14. I Will Be What I Will Be .... אֶהְיֶה אֲשֶׁר אֶהְיֶה
15. Upholder of the Fallen .... סוֹמֵךְ נוֹפְלִים
16. Everlasting Rock .... צוּר עוֹלָם
17. Ancient One .... עַתִּיק יָמִין
18. The Presence .... הַשְּׁכִינָה
19. The Place .... הַמָּקוֹם
20. Holy One of Israel .... קְדוֹשׁ יִשְׂרָאֵל
21. The Name/The Essence .... הַשֵּׁם
22. Shield of Abraham .... מָגֵן אַבְרָהָם
23. The One .... אֶחָד
24. The Truth .... אֱמֶת
25. Creator of Heaven and Earth .... קוֹנֶה שָׁמַיִם וָאָרֶץ
26. YHVH/Causes To Be .... י-ה-ו-ה
27. Former of All .... יוֹצֵר הַכֹּל
28. Shepherd of Israel .... רוֹעֵה יִשְׂרָאֵל
29. Maker of Peace .... עוֹשֶׂה הַשָּׁלוֹם
30. Beloved of Israel .... אוֹהֵב אֶת עַמּוֹ יִשְׂרָאֵל
31. Designer of Creation .... עוֹשֶׂה מַעֲשֵׂה בְרֵאשִׁית
32. Guide .... הַמֵּכִין מִצְעֲדֵי גָבֶר
33. Support of the Righteous .... מִשְׁעָן וּמִבְטָח לַצַּדִּיקִים
34. The True Judge .... דַּיָּן הָאֱמֶת
35. The Good One Who Does Goodness .... הַטּוֹב וְהַמֵּטִיב
36. The Sustainer of Life .... מְכַלְכֵּל חַיִּים

GOD, THE LESSON PLAN
For middle elementary through older teen aged groups

This unit repeats some of the teachings in the Four Worlds Lesson Plan and in the Shiviti Breath Meditation. Introduce the discussion with the paragraph below. Explore the students' God-concepts in an open and non-judgemental fashion.

> **LEADER:** *In this unit, we will explore common God-concepts of the Jewish people. Some of us may not have much of a God-concept, but ask young children. They'll tell you! God is a very enormous man who lives in the sky. He has a very long white beard and He is normally very gentle. But do not get Him riled up. He can be powerful and vengeful as well.*
>
> *This is called the Zayde Theory of God. Most of us outgrow it by around the 6th grade, but we generally replace it with... nothing.*

DISCUSS:

What are the attributes of the *Zayde*-God. Are any of them useful or meaningful to a more mature person?

What did/do your parents believe about God? God may be the one topic that makes parents of teenagers more nervous than the other three-letter word. Adults seem to feel that they need to "believe" the "right answer." Our opinion is that you can, in fact should, feel your own way to a satisfying God concept.

Does anyone in your group have a God belief or opinion? Can you put it into words? How would you describe God or God's qualities? Does God relate to humans? Now? In the past? How? When do you feel that closeness? Do any of your beliefs correspond to siddur or biblical images?

Continue the lesson by presenting and discussing the concepts below and continue with the discussion questions:

God, The Lesson Plan

1. God is One.

This works pretty well with the Jewish and the scientific approach!. Everything all added up, everything we can see, plus everything we cannot, that ever happened or that ever could happen, plus everything else = God. It is one. Even on the simple physical, historical level, you exist in the same universe as quarks, Venus, the Big Dipper, Galileo, dinosaurs... We're all connected. The Shema is adamant on this point.

2. As Above, So Below

This idea is a bit of a brainteaser. Have fun with it. If you "get it," it's likely to roll around the old cranium for quite a while.

Think about life as a series of repeating patterns. What is true on a very large scale is also true on a very small scale. It's like broccoli. Look at a big stalk of broccoli. You have a trunk with little branches and leaves. Now break off a branch. What it looks like is a littler tree trunk, with little branches and leaves, and so on.

Here's a fun one. Consider the smallest building blocks of your body. Atoms are little wads of energy spinning in circles around each other. So is our solar system. So is our galaxy. So the whole darn universe is little balls of energy dancing around each other. Cool, eh? As above, so below.

3. As Above, So Below, the Sequel

The following insight is from Kabbalah, the Jewish mystical tradition, which some rabbis decided one is not supposed to study until the age of forty... So memorize this lesson and then eat the book.

Here's the deal: Humans have four basic "centers" or functional spheres. We are actually the intersection of four kinds of material: physical, emotional, mental and spiritual. This idea is very widespread in the world's religious and symbolic systems. A parallel symbolism, for example, is earth, water, air and fire (in that order). The sections of the morning prayers go through the four worlds. The early prayers wake us up into our physical awareness. We then go into the Psalms, which are full of emotion and love. Next, the Shema and the many words and thoughts of the Amida prayers place us, mentally, in our context in the universe. The personal prayers at the end (such as

Tachanun) and the Aleynu/closing prayers talk about transformation into the messianic era, ideas from the fourth world of spirituality.

A person can pray in four worlds. You can pray in the physical, just saying the words without any feeling. You can add a real emotional connection with the words. You can think about what you are saying, what it means to use your mind and heart to speak the words. When your mind, heart and body are all doing the same thing, it is spiritual. It feels great.

You probably have experiences in your own life, of times when you were "doing the same thing in all four centers." These moments can be very brief but very meaningful. On the other hand, you also have the experience of "Going through the motions" or feeling something but never acting on it, and so on. When our mind, heart and body are not doing the same thing (i.e. we feel pressured to do something we don't like very much...) it can be very draining. It feels as if we are a broken vessel.

Discussion

Discuss this idea. Give examples from your own life of times you felt totally engaged in what you were doing. Also, think about times you were aware of being at odds inside. Is there a way to involve "all four centers" more of the time? Is that a good idea? Why or why not?

4. God as Punisher

There is a persistent theme in our tradition that God punishes us if we are bad. The idea that God rewards good and punishes evil is found in most religious traditions. It is also very true that there are seemingly evil people who live comfortable "unpunished" lives and very decent people who suffer in ways that seem unfair to us. People have tried to understand this problem for centuries. One way of looking at this problem of reward and punishment is to say that really there is no direct punishment for individual deeds; there are consequences. God does not sit around in heaven saying "83 people broke that commandment. Time for a drought!" But, God, as Universal Law, does respond to "sins." If we do not observe the mitzvah of providing for the needs of the poor, we will live in a society wracked with greed and violence. If we do not rest on the Sabbath or stop to appreciate the splendors of creation, we will live in a world of acid rain and drought. If we do not operate a judicial system which is fair for all citizens, we will create rage and suffering for the victims of that unjust system. It isn't a punishment, it's an outcome.

5. God's Names

God has many names. Some of them may be a little hard to relate to. God as King or Master may not be very appealing in a 21st century feminist democracy! But these are two of many labels and aspects with which we name God. How about God as Healer? Or Orderer of the Universe (pretty much what King is about), or God as Unity, Maker of Light, Slave Freer, Source of Wisdom?

Our personal favorite God name is YHVH, usually written as two yuds and pronounced as Adonai. This name is actually a verb, the verb to be. YHVH contains all the consonants needed to spell Was-Is-Will Be. So "Existence" is one of the God's names.

This name of God is also a breath meditation. For yud, inhale into the mouth and nose. The first heh is the filling of our lungs and torso. The vav is the long oxygen path of our circulatory system. The final heh is a deep full exhale. Try doing this smoothly a few times, holding the shape of each letter in mind as you follow its course through your body.

These four letters also parallel our four centers. The tiny yud is our small but powerful spiritual life force. The heh, made of two lines, is our mind, its ability to sort and decide. The long vav down the center is our torso, our feeling center and the final heh is our physical side, our two feet on the ground.

We truly are made in the image of God!

Mitzvah: The Lesson Plan
For middle elementary through adult

The word mitzvah is usually translated as good deed or obligation. Both are correct. But playing with the Hebrew letters yields a nuanced and interesting sentence based on the meaning of the letters.

מ **Mem**: Mem at the beginning of a 4-letter word is a grammatical device which indicates that the word coming up is a kind of tool. The word for refrigerator, for example, is composed of a mem and then the Hebrew word for cold, so a refrigerator in Hebrew is "a tool that makes cold."

צ **Tzadeh**: Looks like and sounds like "all spread out." A branching tree ends with this letter. The Hebrew word for "fringes" (צִיצִית) has two of them.

ו **Vav**: Looks like and means "hook" or "connect." The Hebrew prefix for "and" or "with" is a vav.

ה **Heh**: This letter has lots of meanings, but its basic sense is breath. It sounds like a breath. Heh looks like an open throat. There are two heh's in the words love (ahavah) and the four-letter name of God. So one meaning of heh, then, is "God in our lives" or "God in our breath."

Now put it all together: מִצְוָה

Mitzvah means: A tool that helps us gather our energy into a focussed awareness of the presence of God in our lives!!!

This "translation" gives us something between a good deed, which is something optional, and a command (God, the law giver in the sky, bossing us around) A Mitzvah helps ME. It helps me remember what I am doing here, and to use my time consciously. We each do the mitzvot we are drawn towards the one we need to do next. Some of us need to rest more (try Shabbat) or work with food discipline (try kashrut) or become more assertive. Lucky us! We have 613 paths to self-awareness. And the way of mitzvot – halachah - means, the Way or the Path or the Journey.

INTEGRATING THE EXERCISES INTO YOUR SYNAGOGUE
A SAMPLE SERVICE

We have offered many tools for developing spiritual awareness in this text. How do we bring this depth and this insight back into the davenning for ourselves and our communities? In truth, this is an enormous experiment on which we have all embarked together! The answers will unfold for us as we do this work.

One part of the answer is that spiritual insight has durability. Once a certain insight or feeling is connected with the words of a prayer, because of a meditation or a life experience, it is quite easy to evoke that memory in a davenning. Deep prayer builds, like pearls on a necklace. As we do these exercises, we and our students begin to have pearls, waiting for us, sprinkled throughout the siddur.

Some of the exercises can be embedded in a service, with a minimum of instructional time. Kavanot, short introductions and explanations can be inserted into a traditional service with relative ease. Some of the experiences that require instruction may be learned during class time and then utilized in a service. Other experiences in this text may be undertaken in an instructional setting. The student or worshipper can subsequesntly bring the depth or insight with them into future davenning experiences. In services that are educational in nature, more latitiude for instruction or creativity may be possible.

A sample "creative" service follows, with some instructions on incorporating the creative parts with dignity and smoothness. The evolving custom, in summer camps and other settings that have incorporated some of these activities into davenning, is to insert the more creative pieces into the early part of the service. The halacha discourages us from mundane speech between the beginning of the Barchu until the end of the Amidah prayer. If a tone of depth is set in the early part of the service, the benefits will often be enjoyed and felt throughout.

In addition to the various exercises we have planted into this sample creative service, the simple tool of a brief introduction before a section of the tefilah can educate a community. A sentence or two can also constitute a smooth transition and provide a reminder for the community about kavannah.

A Sample Service

A Shabbat Morning Creative Service Outline

1. Breathing/Centering - Use instructions for the Relaxation Breathing meditation on page 28.
2. Mah Tovu - Sing in the traditional round or use simple gathering meditation in the Mah Tovu section, page 48.
3. Elohai Neshama - Teach Rabbi Shefa Gold's song (on page 52) from the tape and breathe quietly for a few moments.
4. Birkot Ha-shachar - Invite the group to stand in a circle and use the instructions on page 56 to lead the group in the free form brachot.
5. Birchot Ha-torah

Recite the bracha together "...la'asok b'divrei Torah." Tell the group that today each of them is going to be a source of Torah as well as a recipient of Torah. Break people into logically sized groups (3-5) and ask them to scan the sayings on page 51. Each participant should choose the teaching that seems especially meaningful to him or her. Give them a few moments to find their favorite teaching. Now ask them each to share that teaching with the group and to say why it seemed like a good lesson to them. Gather the group's attention back together by singing a niggun or a song about Torah.

6. Kaddish - Introduce the Kaddish as a moment that is a sort of pause in the service. How were you feeling when tefilot began? What are you feeling now? Give the group a moment to notice any new understandings that came to them so far this day. Lead the Kaddish in a slow chant cadence, with feeling.

7. Baruch She-amar

Teach each of the three parts of the song (instructions on page 62). Fine-tune the singing and add the kavannot. The first group is expressing grounded, earth energy. The second group is singing for the various species and eco-systems. You may want them to say which animal or which part of nature they are expressing. The third group, which musically goes up and down, represents humans. We too have our ups and downs! Allow a few minutes after the chant to feel the energy in the room.

8. Cacophonous Davenning to Ashrei - Sing your instruction to this next section in whatever little tune you feel.

A Sample Service

> *LEADER: This next Psalm is a poem; we'll sing a personal song today; all of us together but all of us at our own pace... Each of us can find our own tune... We can chant together in English or in Hebrew...*

Then, in your own tune, begin to chant the psalm itself. A nice cacophony will develop as people move at their own pace through the prayer.

9. Barchu and Yotzer Or - Traditional

10. Introducing Rabbah Emunotecha - (Sample transition:)
    > *LEADER: That force, that life in all worlds is loving us this very minute, hugging us with gravity, fueling us with oxygen, providing for all our needs. How great is that love. Feel that love pouring into you as we sing Rabbah Emunotecha.*

11. Three Part Shema - Instructions on page 78
12. Three paragraphs of the Shema - traditionally;
13. Witnessing: See Gaal Yisrael lesson plan, page 95. To close:
    > *LEADER: The wisdom and strength that pulls us to our freedom comes to us in so many ways! Baruch atah Adonai...Gaal Yisrael.*

14. Use the walking meditation to introduce the Amidah (page 103).
15. Amidah: Traditional
16. Say a traditional kaddish shalem and the introduction to the Torah service.
17. Torah Service - Suggestions for thematic Aliyot are found on page 147.
18. Healing Circle (page 133)
19. Sing a happy song or the traditional poem as the Torah is being put away.
20. Kaddish & Musaf, traditional.
21. Aleynu Circle - Traditional or exercise from page 149.

Close with the kavanah for the Kaddish Yatom and a traditional Mourner's Kaddish.

Transitions: Some Secrets of the Trade

Once you have a good outline in mind, go over it again and feel for yourself how it will be to move from one section to the next.

Perhaps a sentence or two is in order.

For example: Between the Call to Prayer/Barchu and the Blessing on Light/Yotzer Or.

You want to move people from a creative version of the Barchu/Call to Prayer to the experience or awareness of light and illumination. A simple transitional sentence might be "Look around for a moment and see the light in the eyes of each member of this group. This light and the light of the breaking morning is the light for which we give thanks in Yotzer Or, page 36."

Sing the instructions

Using the same tune as the most recent prayer, chant your brief instructions to the next section.

Example: Movement from Kaddish Yatom to a creative Aleynu

After the kaddish, chant: Holy One, we are so grateful for the healing you have granted those of us who mourn. We pray for the point in time when your healing will touch all humanity. We gather this morning in a circle, to envision that time… (give specific instructions according to the way you want to do Aleynu)

Deepen the Experience

The transition between one section and another can allow a moment to digest the experience of one section before moving on to the other.

Example: Let's say you have just finished a chanting and silence using Elohai neshama and you want to move on to birchot ha-shachar.

LEADER: Continue to breathe deeply. Notice your weight in the chair and your posture. In just a moment we're going to rise for birkot hashachar/morning blessings. Slowly move to a standing position. Feel your feet on the floor. Feel the full expanse of your spine. Breathe fully and deeply. Experience the freedom of motion you have created with your stretches. Good. Continue to breathe fully and deeply as we move into the morning blessings.

The Exercises in Instructional Settings

Communal prayer is bound by both halacha and custom. While the depth of concentration, which is supported by these exercises, might be quite welcome in the average synagogue, the exercises themselves may seem inappropriate or inconsistent with Jewish law. Significantly, for example, any form of interruption (hefsek) between the Barchu prayer (introducing The Shema and her blessings) until the very end of the Amidah is halachically impermissible. Some congregations will incorporate instructions and/or meditations during these times as forms of support for the tefilah, not interruptions. In other congregations, any form of speech that is not davenning will be seen as an interruption. As a prayer leader, teacher or worshipper in these settings, you will need to consult with the custom and practice of your community as you develop ideas about using these exercises in the classroom and synagogue setting.

You will probably find that there is much more latitude when working with children (or in a learner's minyan) than there is in "the big sanctuary." People who are still working on the nuts and bolts of davenning obviously need more instruction; many leniencies are allowed לְשֵׁם חִינוּךְ "l'shem chinuch/for the sake of instruction."

We have observed in our fieldwork that a number of schools and camps have begun to experiment widely with materials and ideas like those found in this manual. In this section, we share some of these models with you.

Typically, these alternative offerings are scheduled for some of the weekly services but not all. Themes are selected *according to the skills and interests of the ba'alei tefilah*/prayer leaders, ensuring that the person offering the elective will be enthusiastic and capable. Students or campers typically are offered choices, assuring that the student will be somewhat invested or at least open to the new or creative aspects of the service.

Camp Ramah in New England has had Alternative Tefilah Days on the non-Torah reading days in the post-bar-mitzvah age groupings since 1993. Commonly these are offered 2-4 times a week, for 2 weeks. In a four week camp session, campers have a chance to try two alternative tefilot, in addition to the "traditional egalitarian" minyanim which are the standard fare at

Ramah. The halacha, as practiced at camp, is that various portions of the early parts of the service were said every day, as well as the Shema and the Amidah. Most of the experimental activities are inserted during the early part of the services and at the closing, leaving the core of the Shema and Amidah intact. Below are some of the descriptions from which the campers chose:

VIGOROUS PRAYER: There is something to be said for appropriate behavior in synagogue, but not here. God is not hard of hearing but that doesn't mean we should be so quiet when we daven. So we will be loud and vocal and shout when we feel so moved.

SPIRITUAL CONDITIONING: Through linking the body and soul, we come to new levels of kavanah/strength of focus in our prayers. Come and find out how prayers can put us in touch with ourselves in new ways.

LET'S COMMUNE WITH NATURE: Explore how nature enhances morning worship. Pray at the most beautiful spots in camp. Combine our prayer with a deep appreciation and wonder.

PRAYER IS POETRY: Let's look closely at the words of the service to listen to their rhythms and enjoy their meaning. A discussion minyan.

FOUR WORLDS PRAYER: Wake up in your body, open in your heart, calm your mind and feel your spirit. Using siddur, chant, trust, breath and gentle stretches, daven in all four worlds.

Solomon **Schechter of Greater Hartford** has a model that is typical of schools electing to offer alternative tefilot. Monday and Thursday, Torah-reading days, there are school-wide minyanim. Friday each grade meets separately and shares some foretaste of Kabbalat Shabbat. For tefilot on Tuesday and Wednesday, students select alternatives for a 6-8 week session. Specific offerings from past years have included:

Tikkun Olam: Themes of World Repair in the Tefilah

Learning the Prayers in American Sign-Language

Bibliodrama: Engaging our ancestors in the Siddur

Meditation and the Mystical Tradition in Prayer

The Exercises in Instructional Settings

At Schechter, as at Camp Ramah, the core of the siddur, Shema and Amidah, are chanted traditionally and the elective themes are generally incorporated before and after the body of the davvenning.

Ezra Academy of New Haven, a Schechter school, has a slightly different model. On Mondays, students are divided into three groups; early elementary, elementary and middle school. Services are conducted with an eye towards skill building and familiarity with the siddur. Tuesdays' tefillot are called "spiritual services;" exercises such as the ones in this manual, stories and other techniques are offered to enhance and deepen the experience of prayer. Wednesday is called Content Day. The upper school students are asked to daven at home; the siddur is studied on Wednesday. Topics include the history of certain prayers, theology, poetry, structure of the siddur and so on. Thursday is a school wide service in the "big sanctuary;" decorum and skill building are emphasized. On Friday, students pray in their classroom and enjoy a foretaste of Kabbalat Shabbat.

These are a few of the many models piloted across North America as we work to help young Jewish people find meaning in and mastery of the siddur.

Gems from the Tradition

When we are asked "Is this meditation new to Judaism?," the following is a sampling of the sources from the Jewish tradition that we use to answer the question.

Moses Maimonides, The Guide of the Perplexed, III:51[16]

The first thing that you should cause your soul to hold fast onto is that, while reciting the Shema' prayer, you should empty your mind of everything and pray thus. You should not content yourself with being intent while reciting the first verse of Shema' and saying the first benediction. When this has been carried out correctly and has been practiced consistently for years, cause your soul whenever you read or listen to the Torah, to be constantly directed -- the whole of you and your thought -- toward reflection on what you are listening to or reading.

When this too has been practiced consistently for a certain time, cause your soul to be in such a way that your thought is always quite free of distraction and gives heed to all that you are reading of the other discourses of the prophets and even when you read all the benedictions, so that you aim at meditating on what you are uttering and at considering its meaning. If, however, while performing these acts of worship, you are free from distraction and not engaged in thinking upon any of the things pertaining to this world, cause your soul after this has been achieved -- to occupy your thought with things necessary for you or superfluous in your life, and in general with worldly things, while you eat or drink or bathe or talk with your wife and your small children, or while you talk with the common run of people. Thus I have provided you with many and long stretches of time in which you can think all that needs thinking regarding property, the governance of the household, and the welfare of the body. On the other hand, while performing the actions imposed by the Law, you should occupy your thought only with what you are doing, just as we have explained.

When, however, you are alone with yourself and no one else is there and while you lie awake upon your bed, you should take great care during these precious times not to set your thought to work on anything other than that intellectual worship consisting in nearness to God and being in His presence in that true reality that I have made known to you and not by way of affections of the imagination. In my opinion this end can be achieved by those of the men of knowledge who have rendered their souls worthy of it by training of this kind.

---

[16] Moses Maimonides, The Guide of the Perplexed, trans. by Shlomo Pines (Chicago: University of Chicago Press, 1963) pages 622-633.

Abraham Abulafia, The Book of Eternal Life, MS Oxford 1582, fols. 51b-53a
Translation by Dr. Ronald C. Kiener

Be prepared for your God, oh Israelite! Make yourself ready to direct your heart to God alone. Cleanse the body and choose a lonely house where none shall hear your voice. Sit there in your closet and do not reveal your secret to any man. If you can, do it by day in the house, but it is best if you complete it during the night. In the hour when you prepare yourself to speak with the Creator and you wish Him to reveal His might to you, then be careful to abstract all your thought from the vanities of this world.

Cover yourself with your prayer shawl and put tefillin on your head and hands that you may be filled with awe of the Shekhinah which is near you. Cleanse your clothes, and, if possible, let all your garments be white, for all this is helpful in leading the heart towards the fear of God and the love of God. If it be night, kindle many lights, until all be bright. Then take ink, pen and a table to your hand and remember that you are about to serve God in joy of the gladness of heart. Now begin to combine a few or many letters, to permute and to combine them until your heart be warm. Then be mindful of their movements and of what you can bring forth by moving them.

And when you feel that your heart is already warm and when you see that by combinations of letters you can grasp new things which by human tradition or by yourself you would not be able to know and when you are thus prepared to receive the influx of divine power which flows into you, then turn all your true thought to imagine the Name and His exalted angels in your heart as if they were human beings sitting or standing around you. And feel yourself like an envoy whom the king and his ministers are to send on a mission, and he is waiting to hear something about his mission from their lips, be it from the king himself, be it from his servants. Having imagined this very vividly, turn your whole mind to understand with your thoughts the many things which will come into your heart through the letters imagined. Ponder them as a whole and in all their detail, like one to whom a parable or a dream is being related, or who meditates on a deep problem in a scientific book, and try thus to interpret what you shall hear that it may as far as possible accord with your reason...

Abraham Abulafia, The Book of Eternal Life, MS Oxford 1582, fols. 51b-53a

And all this will happen to you after having flung away tablet and quill or after they will have dropped from you because of the intensity of your thought. And know, the stronger the intellectual influx within you, the weaker will become your outer and your inner parts. Your whole body will be seized by an extremely strong trembling, so that you will think that surely you are about to die, because your soul, overjoyed with its knowledge, will leave your body. And be you ready at this moment consciously to choose death, and then you shall know that you have come far enough to receive the influx. And then wishing to honor the glorious Name by serving it with the life of body and soul, veil your face and be afraid to look at God.

Then return to the matters of the body, rise and eat and drink a little, or refresh yourself with a pleasant odor, and restore your spirit to its sheath until another time.

Rabbi Kalanymous Kalman Shapira[17]

From Bnai Machshavah Tova
Translation by Andrea Cohen-Kiener

Approaching God

Now, if we should try first to achieve holiness, it will not be within our ability, so we will return to our technique of descending to the grounded body of a man and we will ascend from there. So let us begin with mundane arousal! As we have said, all arousal, even of a physical nature, is a portal to the soul. This can be likened to a man whose son is accused of a crime and imprisoned. He is unable to see his son unless the guard opens the prison and goes in to check on his case. The poor father, since he was let in only for legal advice, speaks to him only of the legalities. But a wise man says "Indeed, the prison guard let me in, but in any event, the door is open! And my son is right here. I will embrace him and kiss him and tell him that I love him." Any strong feeling regarding mundane matters contains a spark from the soul. But in this way, the soul is revealed just a bit. So let us try and extract her further and woo her with words of love and awe and pure thoughts of the Holy One. And even though mundane excitement touches and expresses a bit of the soul, we have then in our hands a tool with which to begin, a way to knock on our heart's doors and call her to come out of the iron gates which bind her. "Open for me, my sister, my love." (Cant. 5:2) Come, let us worship the Holy One, a work which is pure. Let us feel and embody our worship, with faith, love and awe of the Holy One. Anyone who has had a disturbing experience, wherein either himself or someone near to him was effected in some way, God forbid, currently, whenever he remembers and imagines the situation in a strong way, it seems as though it is happening again. His heart melts, he even cries. You too can imagine this sort of situation so you will wake up and become agitated, so that a broken-heartedness overtakes you. "And why should I break my heart and cry over fantasies? Is not God before me? Am I not now standing before the His glorious throne, be He blessed? I will weep before God who hears the sound of weeping." And by using the form of imagination referred to by the Ravad, may his memory be a blessing, which we spoke of before, you perceive more and more how

---

[17] Rabbi Kalanymous Kalman Shapira is also known as the Aish Kodesh and the Rebbe of the Warsaw Ghetto. He was a teacher and Rebbe during World War II. He perished in a labor camp in 1943. Jason Aronson: North Vale, NJ has published many of his writings <u>Conscious Community</u> (1996), <u>To Heal the Soul</u> (1995), and <u>Holy Fire</u> (1994) in English.

you now ascend before the throne of glory, before Him, be He blessed, and you are able to pray and plead. You will see that this method greatly strengthens your prayer. And if you are unable to stimulate yourself by means of some past anxiety, follow the advice of the Gemara: "Remind him of the day of his death." But not in some vague and general way. The Gemara states: "The evil ones know…," but this is their shortcoming, that they just "know"; a vague awareness that does not break the heart with its specificity. Imagine the fate which awaits every man at the fulfillment of his days and years. He will look out, in his last moments, at all the world and his children and he must leave them. His body will go to dust and rot and worms. And his soul must go to an unknown place by an unknown way. His children will surround him and cry and wail: "Oh, Father, Father!" His loved ones and family will groan and cry for him. He can hear and understand everything but be unable to help at all. He sincerely wishes to live but his heart is beating wildly and his throat tightens. He is choking. By force, his soul is rent from his body and heart. And so later, as he is taken to his eternal rest, one of his sons beats his head on the wall and cries "Father, Father, how could you leave us? Where have you gone?" A daughter throws herself on the ground and cries out bitterly "I cannot live without you my Father. I wish I could die in your stead." Tears and cries stream out of her until it seems that, God forbid, she is ready to explode from the despair and anguish bursting out of her. Their cries shake the living and the dead. The whole community groans with crying and pity for him and them. A whirl of confusion and sobbing surrounds him. And at long last they all go home and he is left; and with whom is he left? Specifically, when you read the Reshit Chochmah, Zohar and midrash on what transpires for him and his soul after death, one's heart will surely melt, even a heart of stone. And from this bitterness and emotion, one comes to a desirable frame of mind for prayer as we have described. He will lack neither arousal nor attention; neither faith, love nor fear of God.

GUIDED MEDITATION BEFORE PRAYER AND CHANTING TECHNIQUE

Take for yourself some phrase of a tune, turn towards a wall, or simply close your eyes, and once again, imagine that you stand before the throne of glory. With a broken heart, you have come to pour out your soul to God, with the song and melody that emerge from within your heart. Eventually, you will sense inwardly that your soul has come forth in joy. Even if at first it was you serenading your soul to awaken her from her slumber, little by little you will feel that your soul has started to sing by herself.

It was always a riddle to you, this music. What are notes? What are ascending and descending notes? Why are they sometimes long and sometimes short? But now you comprehend that, with voice, the soul cleaves a way on high. And in heaven, it is as if you are grabbed by the soul's sound and drawn up by the tongue. The heart, guts and subtleties are drawn out by song. And along with the notes, they rise. So the rise and fall and all the intricacies of the notes' pattern is etched, the movement of the melody is inscribed, the tune is woven and the soul takes up the tune to pour it out before the Holy One.

At times, you will unconsciously utter some words before God, perhaps at first concerning material needs, the more you deepen your feelings, the more the soul emerges from her constraints to fly upwards. To that extent, you leave this world and from the depths of your heart, your soul utters true prayer to the One, such as this: "Master of the world, in heaven have mercy on me and help me in all my affairs. Oy gevalt! I cry out. I am nothing and worthless; Master of the world, save me!" He begins with a plea to help him in all his affairs and he ends with a plea to rescue him from his lowly condition, and this is the normal progression. Do not belittle such words for they hew open the soul.

Still there will be times when words will not arise in you and no plea is felt, but even so, you will feel something, which you cannot quite describe. It is a sort of yearning, like a lad who whimpers to his father. He does not want a thing from his father, he simply coos and sighs "My Father, my father." The father asks "What do you want, my son?" "Nothing," he responds. However, he starts again to coo and sigh "My Father, my Father." Be aware that in regard to bringing out the soul, we have many occasions to learn from children. A child's activities are not premeditated. Rather, of its own accord, the soul manifests in various ways, so the child moves and acts in accordance with his soul; and this cooing is his soul pouring towards the soul of his father. You too will occasionally feel in your tune a kind of flowing and reconciling, without speech, without articulation and without any plea; just your soul, happy, flowing and uttering: "Ribboyno shel Olam, Ribboyno shel Olam..."

Selections from Rabbi Abraham Joshua Heschel[18]
God in Search of Man

God is waiting for man to seek Him. "The Lord looked forth from heaven upon the children of man, to see if there were any man of understanding that sought him" (Psalms 14:2). "In thy behalf my heart hath said *"Seek ye My Face..."* (Psalms 27:8). And on the Days of Awe, we recall in humility: "Until the day of man's death, Thou waitest for him to return..." (page 30)

Among the many things that religious tradition holds in store for us is a *legacy of wonder.* The surest way to supress our ability to understand the meaning of God and the importance of worship is *to take things for granted.* Indifference to the sublime wonder of living is the root of sin.

Modern man fell into the trap of believing that everything can be explained, that reality is a simple affair, which has only to be organized in order to be mastered. All enigmas can be solved, and all wonder is nothing but "the effect of novelty upon ignorance." The world, he was convinced, is its own explanation, and there is no necessity to go beyond the world in order to account for the existence of the world. This lack of wonder, this exaggeration of the claim of scientific inquiry, is more characteristic of writers of popular science books and of interpreters of science to the laymen than of the creative scientists themselves...(page 43)

All creative thinking comes out of *an encounter with the unknown.* We do not embark upon an investigation of what is definitely known, unless we suddenly discover that what we have long regarded as known is actually an enigma. Thus the mind must stand beyond its shell of knowledge in order to sense that which drives us towards knowledge. It is when we begin to comprehend or to assimilate and to adjust reality to our thought that the mind returns to its shell.

...Any genuine encounter with reality is an encounter with the unknown, it is an intuition in which an awareness of the object is won, a rudimentary *preconceptual* knowledge. Indeed, no object is truly known, unless it is first experienced in its unknown-ness.

It is a fact of profound significance that we sense more than we can say. When we stand face to face with the grandeur of the world, any formulation of thought appears as an anticlimax. It is in the awareness that the mystery which we face is incomparably deeper than what we know that all creative thinking begins… Religious thinking is in perpetual danger of giving primacy to concepts and dogmas and to forfeit the immediacy of insights, to forget that the known is but a reminder of God, that the dogma is a token of His will, the expression of the inexpressible at its minimum. Concepts, words, must not become screens; they must be regarded as windows…It is not from experience, but *from our inability to experience* what is given to our mind that certainty of the realness of God is derived. It is not the order of being but the transcendent in the contingency of all order, the allusions to transcendence in all acts and all things that challenge our deepest understanding.

Our certainty is the result of radical amazement, of awe before the mystery and meaning of the totality beyond our rational discerning. Faith is *the response* to the mystery, shot through with meaning; the response to a challenge which no one can forever ignore. "The heaven" is a challenge. When you lift up your eyes on high, you are faced with the question. Faith is an act of man who *transcending himself* responds to Him who *transcends the world.* (pages 114-117)

---

[18] Abraham Joshua Heschel, God in Search of Man (Noonday Press, 1987; Reprint edition, Northvale, NJ: Jason Aronson, 1997).

Tefilah Resources

Posters:

National Jewish Outreach carries clear educational posters, good for congregational and classroom use, easy company to work with; 1-800-44TORAH, 485 5th Avenue NY 10017.

Helpful Books:

Worlds of Jewish Prayer, Weiner & OmerMan; Jason Aronson; North Vale, NJ 1994; a collection of essays on kavanah and creative rituals from leaders of the renewal trend in Judaism..

Teaching Tefilah, Kadden & Kadden, ARE Productions; Denver CO; 1994; nice basic resource, lots of activities for varied ages.

Jewish Meditation and other materials by Rabbi Aryeh Kaplan, z"l; interesting thinker with profound comments on the text and experience of prayer. Available from Judaica stores. KTAV and Weiser are his publishers.

Jewish Spiritual Practice by Yitzhak Bauxman; Jason Aronson; North Vale NJ, 1995; a compendium of quotes and recommendations on prayer, etc., mostly from Hasidic circles.

The Book of Blessings by Marcia Falk, HarperSan Fransisco, 1996. New and lovely. A fluid Shabbat and daily prayer book with poetic Hebrew and English versions of the prayers.

The Meta-Siddur by R. David Wolfe-Blank, z"l. Interesting one-page commentaries that help get the siddur off the page. Loose leaf format. Cutting edge material, c/o Congregation Mkor Or 6556 35th Avenue NE, Seattle WA 60645.

Shir Hadash is the original Pnai Or (Renewal) Siddur, loose leaf format. It is out of print but a sample service derived from it is available from Aleph Alliance for Jewish Renewal for $3@; 7318 Germantown Avenue, Philadelphia, PA 19119, 1-215-242-4074.

Serve the Holy One with Joy, by Rabbi David Zaslow is a fully transliterated siddur, with wonderful notations to aid with kavanah, available through him, 503-482-0088, or shalomrav@aol.com

Jewish Guided Meditation by Rabbi Dov Peretz Elkins. What to, how to, and when to; enjoyable and useful guide; 609-497-7375.

Tefilah Resources

Religious Signing by Elaine Costello, Bantam Books; 1986, includes both Jewish and non-Jewish religious vocabulary, well-illustrated. Very good resource.

Higher and Higher: Making Jewish Prayer Part of Us, by Dr. Steven Brown; United Synagogue of Conservative Judaism, New York City, 1980. A wonderful series of exercises and lesson plans that explore some of the affective and cognitive goals of prayer.

Meditating with Children, by Dr. Deborah Rozman, Planetary Publications, Boulder Creek CA, 1974. This is an *indespensible* resource for teachers who wish to use meditation as a tool for teaching prayer and kavanah to children. Dr. Rozman shares concrete and useful startegies as well as a variety of trouble-shooting techniques.

Tapes & Music

Tara Music (410-654-0880) & **Sounds Write** (619-697-6120): Both good catalogue companies with a wide range including renewal and prayerful music. Music is subjective and there are a lot of wonderful artists out there. Rabbi Shefa Gold and Hanna Tiferet Siegel are recommended in this text a number of times.

Aleph ReSources Catalogue also carries taped music, videos etc. 7318 Germantown Avenue; Philadelphia, PA 215-242-4074.

Jewish Sacred Dance is a tape-book set for people who want to lead simple movements as part of their service. Sold by the artist, Latifa Berry Kropf 804-974-7016.

House of Musical Traditions sells a full range of simple percussion instruments from around the world. For $3-$12 each, you can acquire a basket full of easy to use instruments. 301-270-9090.

Cantor Jack Kessler sells sets of tapes with good straight *"hazzanus,"* the art of cantoring. Very useful for folks who are expanding their range of davenning leadership skills. 215-849-9227.

Dr Saul Wachs has created a set of tapes of the regular *nusach tefilah*/prayer cadence for weekdays, Shabbat and holidays. Available from the United Synagogue Book Service; 212-533-7800, extension 2003.

Reb Laibel Wolf is a Lubavich educator with a good manner of conveying meditations and theoretical framework for good prayer. A catalogue of his materials (good quality audio and visual tapes) is available from his American distributor, Raitman, 6445 Sacramento Avenue, Chicago IL, 60645.

Otiyyot Khayyot is a little known "Jewish Tai Chi" system based on the shape of the Hebrew letters. This is a great little tool for antsy kids and kinetic learners as well as meditation oriented adults. Videotape (and workshops) available from Reuven Modek, 215-242-3248.

Healing & Hospice

Often our need to pray is stimulated by illness and loss. Do yourself a favor and get on the mailing list of **The Outstretched Arm,** the newsletter of The National Center for Jewish Healing, 9 East 69th Street, NY NY, 10021; 212-772-6601.

Human Resources

Bibliodrama is a great technique for creative Torah study. Summer residential training programs, local seminars & other resources are available from the Institute for Contemporary Midrash;. 7318 Germantown Avenue, Philadelphia, PA 19119-1795; phone: 215-247-8655. Fax 215-247-9703. Email midrash@aol.com; www.icmidrash.org.

Jewish Meditation Teachers Network is a clearinghouse and network for the 200 or so self-identified teachers of Jewish Meditation. They do not offer acreditation at this time, but are planning regular regional gatherings and conferences. For further information, contact Nan Fink c/o Chochmat HaLev, 2525 8th Streeet, Suite 113, Berkeley, CA, 94710.

An audio-tape of ten of the songs and 5 meditations from <u>Karov L'chol Korav: For All Who Call</u> is available from Melton Research Center for Jewish Education, 3080 Broadway, NYC, NY, 10027.

ABOUT THE AUTHORS

Jeff Hoffman is the rabbi of a Conservative synagogue, Congregation Sons of Israel, in Upper Nyack, New York. He has also been teaching and writing in the academic world of Jewish Studies and has taught at the Academy for Jewish Religion and at various educational and rabbinic conferences and seminars. He holds a doctorate in Hebrew Literature in the field of liturgy from the Jewish Theological Seminary of America. In his spare time, he enjoys playing electric guitar in a rock 'n roll band.

Andrea Cohen-Kiener is a teacher, author, translator and guide. She is the spiritual leader of Congregation Pnai Or of Central Connecticut. She has taught prayer and spirituality in Hebrew Day Schools, camp settings, supplementary schools, highs schools and retreat settings. Andrea is the translator of Conscious Community: A Guide to Inner Work (Jason Aronson, 1996) a Hasidic text on mindfulness and meditation by Reb Kalanymous Kalman Shapira. She is active in the women's movement and in interfaith and reconciliation dialogue.